The Diary of a Rowing Tour

from
Oxford to London
via
Warwick, Gloucester
Hereford & Bristol
August 1875

Howard Williams

ALAN SUTTON
1982

Alan Sutton Publishing Limited
1/a Brunswick Road
Gloucester

First published 1982

British Library Cataloguing in Publication Data

Williams, Howard
  **The diary of a rowing tour from Oxford to
London in 1875.**
  **1. Inland navigation — England — Correspondence,
diaries, etc. 2. Boats and boating — England
— Correspondence, diaries, etc. 3. Rowing
— England — Correspondence, diaries, etc.
I. Title**
  914.21   DA645

  ISBN 0-904387-69-0
  ISBN 0-904387-70-4 Pbk

Typesetting and origination by
Alan Sutton Publishing Limited.
Photoset Caslon
Printed in Great Britain
by Page Bros. (Norwich) Limited.

Contents

Taken at Sydney Gardens, 14 August 1875. From left to right: Eustace Clarke, Tom Williams, Howard Williams, George Williams and Fred Broad. *See* introduction p.7.

Introduction

by Alan Sutton, with prefatory biographical notes by Felicity Catmur.

Howard Williams was just twenty-one at the time of the rowing tour. Brother George was twenty-five, and brother Thomas probably between the two. Regarding Eustace Clarke and Fred Broad, their friends, nothing is now known other than that which appears in the text. For Howard this was probably his first taste of freedom, having reached his coming of age only five days before setting out.

Howard, Thomas and George were born in Greenwich and had one older sister. Their father, George Williams, was a tobacco merchant of reasonable means with two living-in servants. He was already sixty years old when Howard was born in July 1854. By the 1861 census the family had left Greenwich and, so far, it has not been possible to trace where they moved to. From the final lines of the diary, it appears that in 1875 they lived somewhere on the Hammersmith Line. From here on there is no further record of Tom or George except for the diary.

At the age of six Howard was already at boarding school. A letter still exists written to his mother in 1860. Headed only Portsdown House it reads as follows:—

> My dear Mamma, I am very glad to tell you the Holidays will commence on the 14th of this month I hope you will let me come Home I shall try to be a good Boy I am My dear Mamma Your dutiful Son
> Howard Henry Williams.

As his father is not mentioned it seems likely that by then he had died, which may be why the family left Greenwich.

In 1878, only three years after the rowing trip, when they were both twenty four, Howard married Mary Elizabeth Cummings at St. Saviours Church Paddington. She was a singer, with a contralto voice, who later sang at Covent Garden and gave many concerts.

They lived in Bushey and Watford for many years. Howard was one of the founder members of The West Herts Golf Club, Captain in 1895 and Secretary from 1899 for fifteen years. He had a great sense of humour and took part annually in any humorous sketches and plays written specially for the club by a man called Andre. These were published privately, complete with pictures, and a copy still exists at the club.

It seems likely that Howard had private means. The only reference to his working for a living appears on his marriage certificate, where he is referred to as

5

Howard Williams aged about seventy-five.

a 'Clerk'. He does not appear to have had a profession or occupation while secretary of the West Herts Club, when in his forties, so presumably he came into money soon after his marriage. Certainly while on the rowing trip there seemed to be no shortage of money.

Howard's wife, whose stage name was Madame Mary Cummings, died at the age of fifty nine in 1913 at Wimeraux, in France, probably while on a concert tour. They had no children.

Early in 1914 Howard resigned as secretary of the Golf Club. It is not certain, but no doubt his wife's early death had something to do with it and maybe he moved away.

There is no record of what he did during the next fifteen years or so, but he died in 1933, aged seventy nine, at the home of his niece by marriage, in Abingdon. She had looked after him for his last few years.

In his will Howard Williams did not mention his brothers or any member of his own family. Most of his money went in bequests to his wife's relatives. There was also the following bequest:

> To the Captain and Secretary of the Incorporated West Herts Golf Club Watford (of which I believe I am the sole surviving founder) . . . the sum of £50 for the purchase of a Challenge Cup to be inscribed "The Howard Williams Challenge Cup" to be competed for annually

This is still a big event in the calendar of the club. Most of the residue including this diary, which was among his effects, was left to his niece by marriage, Phylis Melwyn Timmins, my grandmother. I therefore believe that it is likely his brothers pre-deceased him leaving no issue.

In turn I inherited the diary from my mother in 1975. I knew it existed but had never really studied it before. Having done so, I felt that, with today's interest in canals and the lapse of time, its historical and social comments plus the charming illustrations should be shared by others. I therefore put all my efforts into finding a publisher and tracing as many of the biographical details of Howard Williams as I could find.

All I had to start with was a copy of his will and a few vague memories of things I had been told about 'Uncle Bill and Aunt Mary'. After much research at the Public Records Office and a visit to the West Herts Golf Club, I have been able to piece together the rather sketchy details above. I now hope that thanks to the publisher Alan Sutton, many people will be able to share this fascinating insight into the Waterways plus the pubs, hotels and beauty spots along their routes in 1875.

FELICITY CATMUR
Epsom 1981

The frontispiece of this book forms part of a title page on the manuscript diary and is surmounted by a hand drawn crest thus:–

There is little evidence for concluding that the lettering relates to their positions in the boat other than the photograph shown above left which, although taken fifty-five years later, shows a facial resemblance to the centre figure. Howard's bouncy self-confidence also shows through in the group picture, with the posed, rakish position of his 'boater'. The internal evidence is based on the line illustration shown on p.101, and the wording on that page, – 'Fred and I, therefore, went across on a raft . . .'. The figures in this illustration show one with sideburns, the other with a moustache and, as only one member of the party in the photograph has a moustache – and looks too old to be Howard, it must be Fred. The photograph shows the central figure having sideburns, the left-hand figure is too out of focus to establish the point. An earlier cameo drawing of Howard illustrated here also shows sideburns; therefore I think the assumption that the crest relates to the photograph is reasonably safe.

Fred Broad is exactly as I visualise Harris in Jerome K. Jerome's *Three Men in A Boat*, the analogy to which it is difficult to avoid in this diary, although it pre-dates Jerome by fourteen years. There are many little touches which put one in mind of Jerome, Harris and George – to say nothing of the dog. The first of these to send me searching for my copy of Jerome was the reference to the steam launch at Banbury Lock.

> . . . there was the usual complement of barges waiting outside, and a steam launch, the occupants of which were much amused at our being stopped on our journey . . .

– and after pleading their case to the lock keeper that theirs was a *special* pass:

> . . . I went back to the boat and we passed through, giving our friends in the launch a parting triumphant grin.

Both Howard and party, and Jerome and friends, were part of the river set. At the very end of the diary on their return to Teddington:–

> Fred the boatman received us, and was rather astonished at our bronzed appearance. We changed our clothes not liking to be seen on Sunday evening going home in our flannels. We left the cans, rollers, winches and flag in our locker.

It is quite possible that Jerome and Howard knew each other, Howard being only five years the senior, however, the 'set' seemed to share an antipathy for steam launches. Jerome:–

> 'Steam launch coming!' one of us would cry out on sighting the enemy in the distance; and in an instant everything was got ready to receive her. I would take the lines, and Harris and George would sit down beside me, all of us with our backs to the launch, whistling, and on we would go drifting. At about a hundred yards off, she would start whistling like mad, and the people would come and lean over the side, and roar at us; but we never heard them! Then that launch would give one final shriek of a whistle that would nearly burst the boiler and she would reverse his engines, and blow off steam, and swing round and get aground . . .

'Why, George, bless us, if here isn't a steam launch!' And George would answer: 'Well, do you know, I *thought* I heard something!'

Later in the book . . .

At Reading Lock we came up with a steam launch, belonging to some friends of mine, and they towed us up to about a mile of Streatley. It is very delightful being towed up by launch. I prefer it myself to rowing. The run would have been more delightful still, if it had not been for a lot of wretched small boats that were continually getting in the way . . .

And they are so confoundly impertinent too . . . you can whistle until you nearly burst your boiler before they will trouble themselves to hurry.

The hypocrisy is amusing and obviously intentional. Times may change, but situation humour does not. We all experience the same hypocrisy in the pedestrian v. driver syndrome – depending on which we are at the time. However, to get back; before we leave the Jerome analogy there is one small passage by Howard that could easily have fallen from Jerome's pen (p.130).

Sitting at the next table to us was a party of three, two gentlemen and a girl, these had ordered a very swell dinner, and they were positively worse off than we were; we only expected a supper and got it after a fashion. They expected a good dinner, and after all, only got the same as we had. It was very amusing to hear the elder of the two men continually pitching in to the waiters; the soup was cold, he said; the fish was salt, the entrées were burnt and the wine was vile. He begged one of the waiters to oblige him by tasting a potato but the waiter, probably knowing more about it than he cared to say, firmly but respectfully declined.

Howard, his two brothers and friends, came from a relatively wealthy middle class background, and an analysis of the expenditure during the trip is interesting. Rail fares and canal passes would have well exceeded £6. 0s. 0d. and if we take Howard's comment about the Cross Keys at Great Bedwyn (p.112) where they *only* paid 14s. 9d. for three (the other two having returned to town by this time) and logically extended this to 21s. being a normal amount for three, then accommodation must have cost them in the region of £28. 0s. 0d. On top of this there was the hire of the boat, the cost of which is not mentioned, and incidentals. All in all the total must have exceeded £40. 0s. 0d. and at a time when coal in London could be bought for 8s. 0d. per ton, or an agricultural labourer's wages were only 15s. 0d. per week, it represents a considerable sum. It would easily have kept a labourer and his family for a year! Certainly the largesse given to countrymen for opening locks would have been gratefully received, and the wharfinger at Heyford, on refusing a tip, caused Howard to remark 'the sort of man you sometimes read about, but very seldom see!' The poor 'unsophisticated' waitress who brought them back a tip of a shilling, not realising that it was gratuitous, is an example of the hardships endured in the rural community, and not shared by Howard and party in their sheltered existence. One can almost feel sorry for the two men at Stafford Mill (Defford Mill?) who volunteered to open the lock, and then lost their tip when the stream carried the boat away too fast. The lock setter on the Kennet and Avon was more lucky – after running along the bank to open the bar locks he went away well satisfied with a shilling.

The party were not averse to good living, for when Fred left to go back to town, Clarke 'stood a bottle of champagne' and later, when Tom met up with the others again at Shepperton, he brought a couple of bottles of champagne, which even at that date was not an inexpensive item.

Once away from the Thames, the boat was the centre of attention in every town and village. At their second stop — Fenny Compton — a 'whole troop of people rushed from the George and Dragon' and at Leamington 'people turned out in greater numbers to chaff', at Hampton Lucy 'the whole population came out to stare', and at Newent a large crowd came to see them. Even at Bath, where you would imagine there to be a boating fraternity, the inhabitants came out in their hundreds, and it was not until they were back in 'civilised' regions on the Thames that they ceased to be a spectacle. Howard refers to pleasure boats when he sees them, but they are nearly always 'antedeluvian' as at Leamington, or the occupants 'duffers — their arms going like windmills' as at Evesham.

Some of the comments made show how drastically life has changed over the last hundred years. At Warwick it appears that many of the houses had shutters and actually did shut them at night and, at 6.30 a.m. the next morning, Howard could get a shave at a barbers. The Land Agent at Warwick Castle was anxious about the social status of those he allowed through on the Avon past the Castle grounds:—

> . . . simply asking us a few questions as to where we started from and so on, to make sure we were Bona Fide travellers, and not from Birmingham, to the people of which place he told us he was very chary about giving permission as they were very rough and knocked the place about.

At Tewkesbury they were surprised the shops shut at 5 p.m. until they were told that they always shut at this time on a Thursday. Many shops stayed open until very late, and at Bath and Bradford-on-Avon, they went to the Post Office to collect their mail — a regular occurrence at every town — well after 6 p.m. At Ledbury they saw a coach from Ross. Obviously in some of the more remote market towns the coaches were still in operation, although the railway even reached here within the next few years.

One of the most valuable shops — where Fred was always to be found — was the photograph shop. It seems that most market towns had one selling views of the area, and many of these views, purchased during the trip, were stuck into the manuscript diary and are reproduced in the text. Another modern innovation was the telegraph. Before leaving the trip to return to his business, Fred sent a telegram to say when he would be home. This could only have become common practice a few years previously, and in the line illustration on p.83, telegraph wires can be seen in the background.

The comments on the canals show that the Oxford was still busy, whilst the Herefordshire–Gloucestershire was all but empty, and within six years it was closed altogether and replaced by a railway. The Upper Avon had ceased to be navigable about two years previously and the locks were either in very bad state of repair or unusable. At Chepstow, although arriving late, they were able to have their boat repaired overnight at James' boatyard! On the Kennet and Avon:—

> . . . there was positively no trade at all between Devizes and Reading, we did not meet a single barge the whole of the distance: between Bath and Devizes, the only reason they use barges is to fetch the stone from the quarries . . . we were told that the Great Western Railway leased the canal.

The line illustrations that appear in the manuscript diary have all been reproduced here. On careful examination they can be seen to be by different hands. There is a reference on Sunday August 1st to Fred making a sketch, and on looking at the illustrations it is easy to see that many must have been made at the time, and not from memory, although Howard does not mention this. Some of the best are Claydon Lock, through the woods at Warwick, Clarke slipping down the bank, and perhaps the best of all, – the entrance to Oxenhall Tunnel. It seems likely that these better illustrations were by Fred as all the good illustrations cease after his return to London. There are at least two, possibly three, other 'hands'; one can be identified at the steps to the Fish and Anchor, another at Charlecote Mill. The George at Newent is initialled 'T.W.' and is therefore a giveaway. Some of these have a stiffness and naivety about them but they all add to the charm of the diary.

Howard was obviously quite well travelled. He knew Banbury to be not very lively – from experience, and when back on the Thames it was definitely back to home territory. The proprietor of the French Horn at Sonning he knew by name, and talked of 'renewing the acquaintance of Spot and his wife'. At the Ferry Hotel 'everything is *always* very good' and at Chertsey 'on previous occasions we had stayed at the Cricketers', so trips up the Thames had been a proving ground for the rowing tour.

The condescension and smugness is sometimes a little irritating. Howard admits to being short measured at Windsor because –

> I discovered, however, that I had been given a quart instead! [of half a gallon]. It was very evident that we were nearing London. It was the proprietor of the shop who served, an awful swell in his way, and because I told him to "hurry up" I suppose he took offence and thought he would pay me out.

This attitude, however, although not mentioned is sensed throughout the diary – p. 117:–

> I got out with the winch, and called out to a man who was standing on the gate to move, as I was going to shut it. He replied that I should not shut it as he had just opened it for his barge which was coming down the canal. We had no time to waste, so I did not argue with this, but shut the gate with him on it, and let down the sluices, while George opened them at the other gate. The individual was greatly incensed at first, and seemed as if he would show fight, but thought better of it, and said he would fetch the lock keeper to us . . .

The diary taken as a whole is a wonderful piece of social history as well as a descriptive travel journal for the waterways of the west of England. When so much is known, seen and read of the great country house, it is good to see how life was seen by a social class one step removed, and to see the descriptions and hazards of the country inns. With the contemporary photographs and line illustrations, Howard Williams' diary provides an enchanting and easy way back to that rainy August in 1875.

ALAN SUTTON
Frampton-on-Severn 1982

Wednesday. August 11th

Got up at 8, had breakfast at 8.30, cold salmon and eggs. Ballinger, our landlord, had baled and cleaned the boat, while we had been breakfasting, so we carried it down to the water, and loaded it, starting away at 9.30. It was a dull morning, and almost imme- diately after we started we had a shower of rain, but the wind was not so violent as on the previous day. We very soon came to the new wear, which we had taken observations of the previous afternoon. This was the longest sheaw we had yet come to, and would have been very dangerous if there had been less water, only fortunately the rocks were well covered. Bal- linger, by way of parting consolation, told us that two years previously, seven fellows had at- tempted to go down in a boat, and the boat had been smashed, and they of course all had a ducking: this was not encouraging for us, but we hoped to do better. Clarke was steering, Toms & Fred were sculling, and I was in the bows: we got way on the boat and

New Wear

A reproduction of a page of the manuscript diary reduced to 75%.

Introductory

The members of our party were Eustace Clarke, Fred Broad, my two brothers George and Tom, and myself, Howard Williams. Our boat was a light pine pair-oared gig, filled with a commodious locker under the stern seat: we hired it from Messenger of Teddington. We all went down some few days before we started, and tried it on the river, at the same time taking it ashore, and carrying it some little distance along the bank, so as to have some idea of its weight — Messenger sent it up on Friday, 30th July, by cart to Paddington Station, where George and I received it, and left it in a place of safety for the night. The following is a complete list of the boat's stores:-

Tow Mast and Line	Two Windlasses
Two pairs Sculls	Five rollers
One pair oars	Box of grease
Paddle Boat Hook	Ball of string
Boat Hook	Lantern
Stern Cushion	Matches
Two Stretchers	Soap
Two Pads	Ordnance Maps
Three pieces matting	Tarpaulin
Two feather Pads	Flag
Bow lounge Board	Rug
Bow Cushion	Spare Cord
Two Cans (1 gallon each)	Dutch cheese
Two Pannikins	Six fenders

The rollers were round pieces of wood, 18 inches long and two inches in diameter; we found them very useful in cases where the boat had to be moved along the ground; the windlasses it was quite necessary to take, as it was the exception to find a keeper at a lock. The trip, we all agreed, was most enjoyable; the country we passed through was a complete novelty to all of us except Fred, and the only thing that detracted from the pleasure was the bad weather which we had for about ten days: against rain, however, we had well provided ourselves.

Saturday, July 31st

My brothers and I got up at six, and Fred came in soon after, and we all had breakfast together: we fetched a cab, and packed George and the luggage in it, started him off, and we three walked down to Paddington Station. The station was crowded with people going off on excursions, this being the Saturday before Bank Holiday. The porters appeared to be awfully busy, and it was some time before we could get them to move the trucks into position: with the help of some of the officials we lifted the boat up, carried it along the platform, and placed it on one of the trucks with the bow stretching over the other, but not touching it: we placed some sacks of straw (which Messenger had sent up) under the keel to prevent it from chafing, and tied it round with string, then put all the sculls and sundries in the truck. We took a ticket for the boat, which cost 37/6d., and our own tickets, bought some papers, got a carriage to ourselves, started at 8.10, and had a very pleasant journey down to Oxford. We saw the effects of the late floods, the county being covered sometimes for miles, and the tops of the hay-cocks in some places appearing above the water. We reached Oxford at 11.30, and found the station in a great state of confusion, crowded with country people evidently going off for their holidays. We waited about in the station for quite half an hour, our trucks being shunted about from one place to another. Eventually we saw them taken off into a siding, so leaving Fred in charge of the luggage, George, Tom and I got hold of two porters, lifted the boat off the trucks, and carried it on our shoulders some little distance along the line to where the railway goes over the River Cherwell; we then went down a little narrow path in the embankment and launched it. Fred soon appeared with the luggage, and another porter with the sculls, cushions etc., and they were all placed in the boat. Fred and George then went into the town with one of the cans to get something to eat and drink, and also to obtain the Canal Pass, without which craft are

5

10

15

20

25

30

not allowed to pass through the locks. George got this at the office, for which he had to pay 20/-, and Fred struck a bargain at a cook shop for some hot meat, which having wrapped up in a nice piece of paper he brought to us; he also bought some new loaves and some milk. In the meantime, Tom and I had not been idle, we had got the boat through a lock into the Oxford Canal along which lay our route; had put everything in order, and had got out the cheese preparatory to the arrival of the bread. On the arrival of George and Fred we partook of a frugal but hearty repast.

The locks on this canal are all closed on Sunday, there being no traffic allowed on that day, and the lock keeper was just going home after fastening the gates, but we stopped him and he waited until we had passed through. We started on our journey at 1.30, there was a stiff breeze blowing, but it was a lovely afternoon with a bright warm sun. We had brought with us a most elegant little flag worked in our colours, blue and white, which had been presented to us before we started. This we stuck up in the bow, but it very soon came to grief, as, after we had gone a short distance, in getting out the tow line, it got foul of the flag pole and snapped in two; however, Fred stuck it up again and although not quite so conspicuous, it answered our purpose very well. When we got to the first lock, we took the boat out of the water, and with the assistance of the rollers we ran it round, but found it uncommonly heavy, especially in getting it up the bank: these locks

we found were all very deep and very narrow. We passed altogether
ten of these, but learnt experience at the first one, and went through all
the rest with the exception of one, when we took all the things out and
rolled it round, but we found that this took up more time than opening
the gates and going through in the ordinary manner: there were no   5
lock-keepers to any of them except the first, but with our winch we
found no difficulty in opening the sluices. Although we were not in the
River Cherwell, we followed its course, there being sometimes only
the tow-path separating the two waters: we were in what is called the
"Valley of the Cherwell," the scenery is pretty, there being abundance   10
of trees, but the river had only a short time before overflowed its
banks, so that the country round was in a somewhat immersed state.
About 3 o'clock we passed through the small village of Thrupp, where
we landed and bought some beer; shortly after we found the way
completely blocked by a barge lying right across the canal. We had   15
great difficulty in getting past this; but the bargees were very civil and
assisted us all in their power, although they could not move their
barge, it having got aground. We went on alternately sculling and
rowing until 7 o'clock, when we reached Heyford, where we had
arranged to stop the night, and where Clarke was to arrive in the   20
evening from London to meet us, he having been prevented by
business from starting with us in the morning.

The Gt. Western Railway keeps almost entirely the same route as
the canal and the River from Oxford to Heyford, and at the latter
place the station is only separated from the canal by a wall and the tow- 25
path. There was a wharf at the side of the water, just beyond the stone
bridge that leads to the village. We saw a man there, who we
afterwards found out was the wharfinger, and in answer to our
enquiries, he told us we might leave our things with him for the
night. We accordingly emptied the boat, and tied it up alongside a   30
large barn door which overlooked the canal, and passed the things into
the barn, where they were locked up. We then took our traps and
walked up the main street to the "Red Lion", the only inn in the place,
and enquired of the landlady whether she could accommodate five. She
stared and appeared nervous, probably she wondered whether her   35
beds would accommodate our entire lengths, but finally, after con-
sulting with her good man, she informed us that she could put us up.
This having been satisfactorily arranged we retired to our rooms and
washed. We ordered supper and then went down to the station to meet
Clarke. His train was due at 7, but he did not turn up until 8; he was   40
very glad to see us waiting for him, as he had been put in a state of

terror of an individual in the same carriage who had told him that
there would be no accommodation at Heyford for five fellows; but we
soon convinced him that that individual was wrong, the resources of
Heyford evidently being more than he had any idea of: we were no
less pleased to see Clarke than he us, for it was satisfactory to get all
our party together. We went back to the inn, and had a capital supper
of ham and eggs, and afterwards the landlord brought us a dish of
splendid grapes, a present from our friend the wharfinger. After
supper I sat for some time in a very uncomfortable position while
Fred took my portrait; we then wrote home, and entrusted the letters
to an old gentleman in the bar who made himself most polite, and
begged us to allow him to intercept the post-cart, and give them to
the postman. It being a lovely night, Tom, Fred and I went out for a
stroll and to have a smoke. We walked up the hill at the back of the
village, and amused those natives who had not gone to bed, with our
songs. It was very pretty along the road, and we enjoyed our walk
immensely: we came back at 10.30, and found George and Clarke
chatting over their grog. We soon turned in; Fred and I slept
together, and George, Tom and Clarke occupied a double-bedded
room. Fred would not go to sleep at first because the sheets were
damp, but when I remonstrated with him, and told him how nice it
was to have damp sheets in such hot weather, he succumbed, and was
soon snoring.

Sunday, August 1st

We got up at 7, and it being a glorious morning, Fred, Clarke and I went for a walk along the tow-path; we passed the village church on the opposite side of the water, a very old place with an ivy-covered tower; there was a large drove of pigs in the churchyard which rushed at Clarke in a most brotherly manner when he called them. We walked for about a mile until we came to a swing bridge, where we sat down and rested, and Fred made a sketch. These bridges go flat over the water, so that boats cannot well pass underneath, but they are easily managed, for one has only to go across and pull the chains — which makes the bridge stand on end, and after the boat has passed, by standing on the edge of the bridge, one can make it swing down again. We returned to the Inn and had breakfast at 8, chops and tea. We made it a rule under ordinary circumstances never to have coffee, as from previous experience in country places, we generally found it come to table either of the substance of soup, or else like pale ale. We filled one can with beer and one with milk, and went down to the wharf, where we found the Wharfinger waiting for us. We packed the boat, and started away at 9.30, the Wharfinger absolutely refusing to accept any remuneration for his polite attention; a sort of man you sometimes read about, but very seldom see. The first two locks we passed through all right, but the third we found was locked; there was a lock-house attached to this, so two of us went in and found a very rheumatic old man who refused to let us through, stating that his orders were not to allow any craft through on Sunday. We showed him our pass, and explained that we should either have to go *through* or *round*. This had little effect, until we said we could recommend our brandy which was very good for rheumatics: we gave him a dose, when he fetched the key, and we went away triumphant. George and I started off in the morning with the sculls, and afterwards Clarke and Fred had a turn with the oars but the canal was almost too narrow for

them, so they soon gave them up. We went through a good many
locks, and often found several barges wedged up against the gates
waiting until Monday; but the bargees were generally very civil, and
moved out of the way to allow us to pass. We arrived at Banbury about
12, and were stopped by a very formidable looking lock situated in the
middle of the town. There was the usual complement of barges
waiting outside and a steam launch, the occupants of which were much
amused at our being stopped on our journey: it was impossible for us
to get round the lock, as there were tremendously high walls on either
side, and a large wharf on the other side leading to another lock also
hemmed in by walls. We were rather nonplussed at this; but I took the
pass, and enquired my way to the Canal Company's Office. I asked for
the Lock Manager, and I was rather unnerved to find I had inter-
rupted him in the middle of his dinner, which is not calculated to
improve anyone's temper. I showed him the pass and asked him to
allow us to go through the locks; but he refused point blank, saying
that his orders would not allow him to do so, and that we should have
to wait until the next day. This would not have suited us at all.
Banbury, I knew from experience, at the best was not a lively place,
but to be imprisoned there on a Sunday afternoon would be more than
I could bear, and besides, if we were detained, it would have thrown
us out in our calculations for the day's routes, which we had, of
course, planned out beforehand. I threatened and entreated the man by
turns, and then told him that our's was a *special* pass. After a deal of
persuasion he finally relented, and said he would go and unlock the
gates. I went back to the boat and we passed through, giving our
friends in the launch a parting triumphant grin, which they returned
with a look of great astonishment at our success. We returned the
Lock Manager's kindness in a measure by rescuing one of his chickens
from drowning, which had fallen into the lock. When we arrived
outside the other entrance we found a perfect mass of barges blocking
the way; it took us some time to get through, but the bargees did all
they could to assist us, and we got into open water safely; but with a
terrible streak of tar all along one side of the boat which had been
rubbed on when squeezing through the barges. In the meantime Fred
and Clarke in fighting for the beer can, had upset it, so George went
into the town to buy some more. We waited a quarter of an hour for
him; but he did not turn up, so I went in search of him. He appeared
directly after I left them, and of course as I could not find him, they
had to wait for me. We pulled alongside the bank on the opposite side
of the tow-path, when we had got about half a mile from the town, and

landed putting the cushions under some trees and had lunch. Our
lunch was not extensive, consisting only of our cheese, and some bread
we had brought away with us in the morning. Each mouthful that we
swallowed was eagerly watched by a large crowd of Sunday School
children, who had collected on the opposite bank, and stared at us with   5
grave interest. We not only afforded amusement, however, to the
infant population, as the crowd was very soon increased by some more
elderly people, amorous couples walking together, and *big* girls, the
teachers, probably, to the before-mentioned open-mouthed infants.
We kept a running fire of remarks at them, and offered to take some   10
of them for a row, and Tom and Fred even went so far as to take the
boat across to fetch as many as it would hold, but modesty forbad, no-
one would accept their overtures. We started again at 4, and very
shortly came to a lock that was fastened up. There was a lock-house,
but on enquiring of a bystander we heard that the keeper had gone for   15
a walk with his family, and nobody knew when he would return;
however, we met him soon after, and he apologised for being absent
from home.

The next two locks were not fastened, but a mile further on, when we got to Claydon, we came to a hill which the canal ascended by means of five locks, all close together. The first and the last of these were locked; there were a good many bargees hanging about, so we got
5 them to assist us in carrying the boat round. About three miles further on we came to what we expected would have been Wormleighton Tunnel. This was marked on the map; but we had been told during the day that the Tunnel had been done away with, and was now entirely open. The channel was very narrow, and the banks on either
10 side very steep: in many places there was not sufficient room to use the sculls properly, so we had to shorten sculls and push through as best we could. After getting through this we sculled on for another three miles and passed Fenny Compton Station which is close by the water, and reached Fenny Compton wharf at 7.30. We had made up our
15 minds to put up at the village for the night, which is about a mile from the water; but fortunately we found there was an inn (the George & Dragon) just opposite the wharf. This was an unexpected pleasure, as it saved us a walk. The road goes over a bridge just at this place, and on our pulling up at the bank, a whole troop of people rushed out of
20 the Inn and stared at us from the bridge. We landed, went in, and enquired whether they had any beds: they replied that they had only two, but could lend us a sofa. We took the boat out of the water, and carried it into a farmyard at the back of the house, locking up the moveables in a barn. The visitors at the Inn all turned out into the
25 yard to examine the boat, as if they had never seen one before. After having tidied ourselves a little, we were shown into supper into an enormously long room which was lighted by two small candles: we did very good justice to the cold beef and eggs which were placed before us, being both tired and hungry after our hard day's work. After
30 supper Tom, Fred and I went for a walk to the village along some lanes, and sang evening hymns. Coming back we saw in the road a magnificent glow-worm: it quite lit up the road and we could see it after we had passed it some distance. We turned in at 10.30; Tom and I had one of the beds, and Fred and Clarke the other. George
35 volunteered to sleep on the sofa in the long room; but he regretted his amiability, for in the middle of the night, Tom and I were awakened by an apparition appearing by the side of the bed, who stated that the sofa in the long room was so confoundedly hard, that he had come to try ours. He lay down on the one in our room, and passed the rest of
40 the night there. Whether he was comfortable or not I don't know; but I noticed that he never again volunteered to sleep on a sofa.

Monday, August 2nd

I got up at 6, went to Fred's room, and pulled him out of bed; we went into the yard, borrowed some mops and buckets, turned the boat on one side, took out the planking, and gave it a thorough good washing. Fred got some oil and rags, and worked hard at the brasswork polishing it, and we altogether got the boat into a very respectable condition. When we had nearly finished, Tom made his appearance and looked on, not wishing to see him idle, we gave him the fenders to pipe-clay, which he did, and put them in the sun to dry. We floated the boat, and got ready for a start before the other two showed up, and then went into breakfast at 7.30 which consisted of ham and eggs. We started away at 8.30, having filled our cans, one with beer and the other with cold tea. The canal hereabouts is on very high land, and winds round Wormleighton Hill; from the tow-path we could see the country for miles round, and the scenery was very fine. We had a nice stretch of water for nine miles, being in the pound. On the canals they call that part the pound, which is at the extreme elevation of the water. After the pound we came to eight locks all close together going down a hill. These were small and narrow, and of course easy to get through, as they take so little time to empty. We saved time, too, as George and I went forward and got them ready, whilst the other three worked the boat through. Soon after this we reached Napton, where we all got out for a rest. We tied the boat up close by the bridge, and Fred and I went to a shop close by and had some milk. I also bought some sugar to put in my tea can. The other three walked to the village and bought some bread and honey, whilst Fred and I picked out a nice shady spot, and lay down and smoked. When they returned, we sculled on for another two miles and arrived at Napton Junction. This is the junction of the Warwick and Napton and the Oxford Canals; one runs into the other at right angles, and just as we were turning the course we heard a shout and saw the lock

keeper putting off to us in a punt from the opposite bank in a great
hurry: he evidently thought we intended slipping through without
paying for our pass, as we had to have another one for this canal. He
was just seeing his wife and family off in a waggon, and he had not
5   seen us until we had got close up. He supplied us with a pass to
Warwick which cost 12/6, and we started along our new road. We
had not gone more than a quarter of a mile before I saw in a field close
by a cow that had just calved. As there was nobody near, I landed and
went back and told the man at the office: he said the cow did not belong
10   to him, but he would inform the owner immediately. We sculled on
for a mile, then stopped for lunch. The ground was very wet and
muddy; there had evidently been some inundations there lately; some
of them lunched in the boat, and Fred and I sat on a stile and ate our
bread and honey. The latter was portioned out in dock-leaves which
15   made capital plates. The man at the office told us we should have
plenty of locks to pass through, and we soon found this to be the case,
for we had not gone more than two miles after lunch, when we came to
a place called Stockton, where there were ten all close one after
another. We got hold of a lockman here who helped us work them,
20   and we got through them all in half an hour, which was very good
work. At Stockton there were a large number of Lime Burners along
the side of the canal. The hands turned out in great numbers to look at
and chaff us — it was here I noticed a board stuck up over a small
shop on which was painted:-

25

```
J. PURGIS
HAY, CORN, BRED
AND COLES
SOLDE HEAR
```

this gives one a good idea of the amount of education possessed by the
30   inhabitants of Stockton. Five miles further on we passed through ten
more locks which brought us to Leamington. This we intended to
have been our resting place for the night, but we found there was no
place to leave the boat, and as it was not late, we decided to push on to
Warwick. The part of the town through which the canal passed was
35   not lovely; the water was very foul and dirty, and the houses at the
sides were miserable little hovels. The inhabitants of these houses
turned out in great numbers to see us pass, and a good deal of chaff
ensued. We were not sorry to get away from the town, as almost
immediately after we came into some beautiful country. The banks
40   were very high and covered with trees. Two miles further on we came
to the end of our journey on the canal, viz. to the aqueduct which

carried the canal over the River Avon. We crossed it, pulled up to the bank, landed and surveyed the place. We expected we should have some little difficulty in getting the boat from the canal to the River, but we were fairly astonished to see what was before us. The river was below us, and to get to it, we should have to lower the boat down an immensely steep bank. We were some considerable time discussing the best means to get the boat down, and eventually decided that the only way would be to lower it with the tow-line. We accordingly stripped it of everything, and fitted the tow-line to the painter. (We should have fastened it to the stern; but there was nothing strong enough to hold by). We got the boat out of the canal, and pushed it over the side of the bank: George, Clarke and Tom held onto the line like grim death, whilst Fred and I scrambled and slipped down the bank, one on either side of the boat to steady it. However, it did not go down with a run as we feared, because the stern being foremost and heavy, the broken uneven ground kept it up, so that Fred and I really had to ease it down sometimes. When we had got it safely down into the field below, we got the rollers, and rolled it for about 50 yards to a sloping bank of the river, and launched it, then fetched all the

moveables and stowed them away. Our proceedings had been watched
from the river by several parties in very old-fashioned rowing boats,
which we afterwards found were hired at a place called Portobello,
near Leamington. Tom and I sculled towards Warwick, and passed
under a magnificent stone bridge built in one span; we expected to
have found a boat-house and landing place when we reached the town,
but the only boat-house we could see was a private one, which was
locked and nobody there. It was a gloomy place, hemmed in with
trees, and a thick mist rising from the water. Right in front of us we
could see Warwick Castle, but between that and where we were there
was a weir barring our way, and with no means of getting round, and
nothing to prevent our going over if we got too near. Fortunately we
spied a man who was fishing from the end of a small garden which ran
down to the water's edge, so we pulled up to him and asked where we
could land. He replied that there was no landing place at all in the
town; the river ran through the Castle grounds and was intercepted by
the weir that we saw, so that no boats should go through. However, he

offered to take charge of our boat for the night, and said that we could
no doubt obtain leave from the Earl's steward to carry the boat around
the weir through the grounds. We accepted his offer, he took the
sculls, etc. into his house, and we started off for the Warwick Arms
Hotel, which we reached at 8.30: we changed our flannels, and had   5
supper, cold beef and eggs. Afterwards Fred and I went to the Post
Office for letters, then, Tom having joined us, we strolled through the
town which is very old-fashioned and uninteresting. The main street is
wide and uneven; at the end of it are some alms-houses built and
maintained by the Warwick family, and connected with this is a   10
church built in a most peculiar manner. It is high up above the
ground, resting on a sort of colonnade which foot-passengers pass
under. There is a very large market place and a very small post office,
and a museum built on pillars. Altogether we were not impressed in a
lively manner with the town. It was a very fine evening, so we walked   15
a little way into the country; coming back we heard some most
charming singing going on inside one of the houses. We applied our
ears to the shutter, and applauded vigorously at the finish. We went to
bed at 11, Tom and I slept together, George and Fred were in another
room, and Clarke was by himself.   20

Tuesday, August 3rd

I got up at 6.30, and as none of the others had turned out, I went for a
stroll and had a shave, also had my hair cut close to my head. I found
this very comfortable; saved the use of comb and brush, and after
bathing, I had only to shake my head and it was dry. Had breakfast in
the coffee room at 8; ham and eggs. We had arranged to spend part of
the day at Warwick to see the Castle, and we also had to obtain
permission from Capt. Fosbery, the Earl's steward to carry our boat
round the weir. It took us some time to collect, as everybody
disappeared after breakfast; but eventually we all managed to meet in a
photograph shop where we bought some views. After this we set out
for the Castle which is close by: the entrance is anything but imposing,
only some large, shabby, wooden gates. We rang the bell, and were
admitted by a toothless old woman; but although not blessed with
teeth, she was blessed with a very considerable power of speech as we
soon found out. On enquiring where Capt. Fosbery was to be found,
she informed us that we could get to his house by crossing the river by
a ferry in the grounds, so we decided to go over the Castle first. We
were going down the Avenue, when the old lady stopped us, and told
us that before going any further we must see the curiosities in the Gate
Room. We accordingly accompanied her into a small room round
which were ranged various implements of warfare, and some immense
staves and tilting-poles, which are said to have been used by the
famous Guy, Earl of Warwick. There was also a horn of the dun cow
that he killed, and the skull of his horse, which appeared to be about
the size of an elephant's. In the centre of the room stood a huge
cauldron, which she said was the family punch-bowl, only used on
festive occasions. The old lady talked away like an automaton,
evidently very well primed in what she had to say. She informed us
that to fill this bowl with punch, it required 18 galls of rum, 18
gallons of brandy, 50 gallons of water, 100 lbs. of sugar and 120

28

lemons, and when full, it held 102 gallons. It is made of bell-metal and silver and weights 800 lbs. We asked her when it had been last used, and she replied that when the present Earl came of age, a large banquet was given, at which time it was three times filled and emptied. She added with a melancholy smile, that on that occasion she got none of the punch herself; there were so many after it that she did not get a chance, as a great many of the visitors got their own share and other people's too. We gave her something for herself and walked down the avenue leading to the drawbridge. This avenue was hemmed

5

in with fine trees, at the rear of which, were high rocky banks, and
from which there was a splendid view of the Castle. We passed over
the drawbridge, and under a heavy iron portcullis, and came out onto
a large lawn; against one of the walls was a target, where we were told
5   by a gardener, Lord Broke, (the Earl's eldest son) practised rifle
shooting. We ascended some stone steps and entered at a side door,
and put ourselves under the charge of a housekeeper or show-woman.
The family was away from the Castle, so we were shown the private
apartments. There were many fine portraits and paintings by van
10   Dyke, Holbein, Murillo etc. and in one of the rooms was a splendid
Venetian marble table inlaid with precious stones, valued at £10,000.
The views from some of the windows were very fine, as nearly all the
private rooms look out onto the river, which runs close under the
walls. Some magnificent cedar trees were also pointed out to us, said to

15   be the finest in the United Kingdom. We went through the dining
hall, which is an immense apartment; the floor is entirely laid with
coloured tiles, being so large it naturally looked very bare, there being
very little furniture in it; but the walls were hung with trophies of war

and the chase. This room was one of those which was burnt at the fire
which took place some years ago at the Castle, and it has been rebuilt in
the original style. The fire-place was enormous, large enough to roast
an ox at. After we had seen everything there was to be seen, we were

shown out, and handed over to a gardener, who led us down some   5
steps in a tower to the ferry. Fred and I pulled ourselves across the
river in the ferry-boat, and made our way to Capt. Fosbery's house,
which is prettily situated in its own grounds. This gentleman was at
home, and we were quickly shown into him, and after stating what we
wanted, he gave us the required permission, simply asking us a few   10
questions as to where we had started from, and so on, to make sure that
we were Bona Fide travellers, and not from Birmingham, to the
people of which place he told us he was very chary about giving the
permission, as they were very rough, and knocked the place about.
We took leave of him, recrossed the river, and rejoined the others who 15
were waiting for us on the bank. We then started, escorted by the
gardener, for the conservatory where there is a large Roman marble
vase, which had been brought over from Italy, where it had been

discovered at the bottom of a lake at Hadrian's Villa, Tivoli. The vase
is of immense height, very beautifully designed, and in almost a
perfect state of preservation. The conservatory in which it stands was
built specifically to receive it. From here we obtained a very extensive
view of the flower gardens, which are very large and kept in perfect
order and condition. We then left the Castle grounds, and outside we
hired a wagonette to take us to Kenilworth, which is about five miles
from Warwick. We had not gone far before the rain, which had
threatened all the morning, came on. We wrapped ourselves up with
rugs and covered ourselves with the carriage umbrella, but it did not
last long. We passed Guy's Cliff House (occupied by Lady Percy),
which is seen from the highroad at the end of an avenue of fine trees,
and on a hill at some distance from us, the driver pointed out the
monument erected in memory of Piers Gaveston, on the spot where he

was executed. We were followed for a considerable distance by a
number of small boys, who entreated us to throw them some coppers.
We only got rid of them by throwing some coins into a brook that we

drove through. On arriving at Kenilworth, we at once went into the grounds of the Castle, in which were a number of visitors. The ruins are very extensive and interesting. We had not been there long before a violent storm came on. We were sheltered for a short time in the grounds, but we decided we had better have lunch in the village while the rain lasted, so rushed across the street to an inn opposite, and had some cold meat and salad. We told the driver to put up his horse and

5

waited for an hour at the Inn until the rain ceased. We then drove
back to the Warwick Arms, changed our things, and walked down to
the cottage where we had landed the night before. We baled out the
boat, and put the luggage in, then pulled across the river where we
5   landed. Some of us surveyed the place and found a spot where we

could launch the boat, pretty easily below the weir. After having taken
everything out, we pulled the boat up the bank, and rolled it for about
50 yards through the trees and bushes to the place we had selected, and
after some difficulty launched it at the bottom of the weir. Whilst
10   shoving the boat along, over the rollers, I accidentally put my foot in a
heap of hot ashes, which I very quickly put out again, but not before it
had made me howl. The boat had been launched in a sort of grotto
where the water was very shallow, so I punted it out into the stream
and sculled a little further down. The luggage was then replaced; we
15   all embarked and started away. Before we had got clear of the Castle
grounds we got in amongst a perfect sea of weeds and reeds which
appeared to stretch completely across the river, but after much

dodging about, we found a small opening near the right hand bank, which we punted through and got into open water. We had no sooner settled well to work, Tom and I sculling, than it began to rain in torrents. We pulled under some trees and got out our macintoshes, leggings and sou'westers, which we put on, and having covered the   5
luggage with the tarpaulin, we resumed our journey. Although the weather was so bad, we could not fail to notice the splendid scenery through which we were passing. The river was wide and very deep, not a weed to be seen: the water almost black, with no perceptible current. On either side were high hills covered down to the water's   10
edge with the most magnificent foliage. We sculled for three miles in the pouring rain, until we were stopped by a weir. The banks on either side were very steep, so we had great difficulty in getting the boat out of the water. Whilst we were removing the things, Clarke slipped on the bank and rolled down, only saving himself from a   15

ducking by clutching hold of the reeds and grass. As it was, he
covered his flannels with a thick coating of mud. We saw two men at
the bottom of the weir fishing, who had caught some splendid pike.

They told us that we should have great difficulty in getting along
further down, as there were many shallows, and the stream was very
rapid, and this we very soon found to be the case; fortunately it had
ceased raining, so we were not hampered with our macintoshes. We
got the boat round, and soon found ourselves in a very different sort of   5
place to what it was above the weir. The river was not above half the
width, and in some places the trees on either bank almost joined
overhead. The river ran so swiftly that at times it was impossible to
guide the boat, and it was so narrow and tortuous that we constantly
stuck in the bushes, and often ran aground. Only a very short time   10
before, there had been disastrous floods in that part of the country, in
consequence of the river having overflowed; hundreds of tons of hay
had been swept away by the water, and carried down the stream. This

had caught and adhered to the branches of the trees, and now that the
water had fallen to its normal height, it was left clinging in large   15
bunches to the branches, ten or twelve feet above our heads. It presented a most extraordinary and fantastic appearance: all the hedges in
the fields also were perfectly clothed with hay. As we progressed, we

found our difficulties increase. Going under Barford Bridge we were
suddenly brought with a violent shock to a complete standstill, having
run aground on a shallow in the middle of the river. Tom, Clarke and
myself immediately jumped out of the boat, and steadied it, or we
should have been over, as the stream was running like a mill-sluice
and carrying the stern round broadside. Fred followed in a leisurely
manner, first divesting himself of his shoes and socks. We managed
after some time to ease the boat into deep water, and all jumped in
again. We were, however, continually running aground, and in each
instance three of four of us had to jump out at once to hold the boat
steady. The stream ran so rapidly, that it was quite as much as one
could do to keep one's legs, and it was hard work for two to prevent
the stern of the boat from being carried round. I was the next one to
come in for misfortune; the boat was suddenly taken by the stream
under a tree which hung over the water, and which was, as usual,
covered with an immense bunch of wet and dirty hay. The others
managed to avoid it, but I was steering, and it completely enveloped
me, covering me with the most filthy stuff from head to foot, and also
making the boat in a dreadful mess. Of course the others immediately
began to roar with laughter at the sight I presented, but their mirth
soon ceased, for we were suddenly swung bow first into the bank, and
wedged broadside to the stream against a fallen tree. We were now in a
predicament; we appeared to be immovably fixed; we could not push
out sideways into the stream as the current was too strong: we all
landed and held a consultation, and Fred and I ran about a quarter of a
mile down the bank to reconnoitre. We found out that we were in the
main stream, and not a backwater, as we thought, and I found out also
that I had cut my instep through treading on something sharp, for we
were both barefooted, having had to be in and out of the water so
often. When we returned and made our report, we decided we would
try what we could do by pulling the boat back by main strength. We
got out the tow-line and attached it to the stern. George and Clarke
took the end of the line, and went further back onto a piece of ground
jutting out into the water. At a signal, they commenced hauling, and
we three in the boat pushed off with boat-hooks with all our strength,
and by this means we managed to get clear. We still had to get through
the rapid, so we refastened the tow-line to the bow, and George and
Clarke having crossed to the opposite bank, guided the boat down-
stream, while Tom and Fred sculled. I held the rudder lines, although
with such a current the boat would not answer to it's helm. This mode
of progression answered very well, and we got through on the second

attempt quite brilliantly. This little episode delayed us altogether three quarters of an hour. George and Clarke ran along the bank with the line quite taut guiding the boat in this way for about 100 yards, which took us through two or three more shallows, and we then stopped and took them in.

After this the river became clearer, although we were often in considerable danger, as the curves in the river were so abrupt and the stream so strong, and there were so many trees and snags to keep clear of. When we occasionally did get into a decent piece of water, we went along at a tremendous rate. The scenery all along continued very fine, although to tell the truth, we had very little opportunity of admiring it. About 6.30 it began to rain again, so instead of attempting to get to Shalford where we had arranged to pass the night, we made up our minds to stop at Hampton Lucy, a very small village, which we found marked upon the map. We sculled up to a weir, which, with a mill, blocked our way, and landed. George and Clarke went into the mill, and enquired whether we might leave our boat there for the night, and having got permission, we cleared the things out. Of course, the matting and cushions were wet through; these we gave to the miller's man, who promised to put them in the bakehouse for the night to dry. Our misfortunes for the day were, however, not over, for, as I was pitching the things out of the boat to Fred, who was leaning over a wall, we managed between us to drop Clarke's bag, containing all his worldly possessions into the water. As he was at the time pretty nearly wet through, it was very unpleasant for him, but he bore it very well, much better than I should have done. While we were stowing the things away for the night, and securing the boat, George and Fred walked into the village to enquire about accommodation for the night. The village is only a scrap of a place, and the inn is to match, not only is it a public house, but it is also a grocer's shop, and when they arrived there they found only one young woman looking after the tap-room, the bar and the shop, so that she had her hands full. Tom, Clarke and I very soon arrived, and finding the others had gone in, we naturally followed. It appeared that the young woman that they saw was not the mistress of the house, and she very rashly promised to do what she could to accommodate them, but when we three others arrived, she was much bewildered, as there were only two beds, and the climax was reached when the landlady herself arrived, who appeared to be of rather an irascible nature. She wanted us all to go away again, but once there, neither her persuasive or threatening powers could move us; eventually when she had cooled down a little,

she said she supposed she must manage it somehow. We therefore
changed our wet things for dry flannels, and soon after 8 we had a
capital supper of eggs and bacon set before us, of which we partook
with much relish. The inn was very clean and comfortable, and I must
say that both the old and young woman treated us uncommonly well,
and made us very jolly and comfortable. There was a sofa in the
parlour, so we tossed who should occupy it. Clarke won, but they
made him up a capital bed. After supper we went out in the verandah,
smoked, and read the papers; then went in and had some grog, and
chatted with two farmers who had come in for a short time. They were
turned out at 10, as also were the occupants of the tap-room, who had
been singing all the evening in a dialect quite unintelligible to us. We
went to bed at 11, Fred and I in one bed, and George and Tom in the
other.

Wednesday, August 4th

George, Fred and I got up at 6, dressed, put on our water shoes, and went down to the mill. It was a very dull morning, with rain threatening; but it soon afterwards cleared up and came out fine. We took the boat across the river, drew it up on the bank, stripped it, and gave it a thorough good cleaning, and not before it wanted it, for it 5 was full of dirt and mess which had collected the day before whilst passing under trees, and pushing through bushes. After we had cleaned the boat, I went across the river in an old flat-bottomed boat belonging to the mill, and which was half full of water, and fetched

the oars, sculls etc. I got the miller's man to make a roaring fire in the bake-house, to dry the matting and cushions, and having got everything ready for a start, we returned to the village.

On our way back to the Boar's Head, we passed the Church, which is a perfect little gem outside; our view of the inside was limited. It did not extend beyond what we could see through the keyhole, as the door was locked. We were told that someone had left a large sum of money to be laid out upon it. We had breakfast at 7.30, the usual fare, ham and eggs, paid our bill, had our cans filled with beer and milk, and turned out in the garden for a short time to have a smoke, and seek what we could devour among the fruit trees. We then left our two hostesses with mutual regrets, (for we had made capital friends with the old lady) and returned to the mill. As we passed down the street, the whole population came out to stare at us. We were special objects of interest to the children, who greeted each fresh arrival with outbursts of enthusiasm. We lowered the boat down the bank into the water below the weir, and fitted the things in, in the course of which George dropped one of the pannikins overboard. As we only had two, this was a loss much to be regretted; we fished about for it for some time, but could not recover it. We started away about 9, and on passing under the stone bridge just below the mill, we found a number of villagers had congregated on it, to see the last of us, and give us a parting cheer. We sculled about a mile, and then came to Charlcote Park, the seat of Sir Spencer Lucy. This gentleman has evidently very little sympathy for rowing men, as just at the boundary of his park, he has had a row of posts sunk right across the river. These were connected by chains, and there was also a row of floating planks just underneath the chain, kept in position by being attached to the posts. This barrier as well as another at the other end of the park, was for the purpose of preventing the deer from swimming up the river, and getting away. We could not get the boat round, as the banks were so steep, and as the chains just touched the water, we thought that if the boat was lightened sufficiently, we might perhaps be able to get over with a rush. Clarke, Fred and I therefore landed, taking the rudder off, and leaving Tom with the sculls, and George in the stern to direct him to the easiest place where the chain appeared to be an inch or two under the water. Tom made a rush at the place, and the boat glided over well, as the bow was well out of the water. It was some little time before we three could get on board again, as the banks were so steep, however, we managed it at last by hanging down over some railings, and dropping in. We very soon passed Charlcote House, a large

Elizabethan mansion, with a broad flight of steps leading down to the water. There was a pretty little waterfall just beyond, where a stream ran into the river. About 200 yards further round the bend, we came to the other barrier, this looked more formidable than the first. Fred, Clarke and I again got out, walked round a copse, and waited on the bank to see the performance. Tom put on a spurt, and rushed at the barrier, but alas! the chain only just touched the water, and as the boat ran against it, the shock made Tom catch a tremendous crab, and he disappeared in the bottom of the boat with his heels in the air: we on the bank roared with laughter, Tom got up and rubbed himself, and George looked indignant. In the meantime the boat was suspended

across the chain, one half on either side, and wobbling up and down in a most uncomfortable manner. We suggested various methods, but eventually George went forward in the bow, and so got the stern light and by dint of pushing and shoving with boathooks against the posts and planks, they managed to get over. Altogether we considered ourselves lucky in getting across so well, and we had no desire to have any more jumps to clear. We had been told that there were no locks on the Avon above Stratford, and this we found to be the case, as at Ford Mill we again had to disembark, and carry the boat round below the weir. After this we went merrily on for 3½ miles with a capital

stream, and through very beautiful scenery, which changed in feature
every few minutes: one minute we went along water that was as wide as
the Thames, and the next found us in what was more like a brook,
with the trees almost meeting above our heads and the stream rushing
5   under us and carrying us along at a tremendous pace round sharp
corners. In these narrow parts the river wound in a very extraordinary
manner, making in some places, almost circles. On nearing Stratford,
we came across the first pleasure boat we had seen since leaving
Warwick. There were two or three with girls in them who stared at us
10   in great amazement. We reached Stratford at 12.15, sculled under the
old stone bridge, and landed at the place where they let out the few
pleasure boats that belong to the town. The first thing we saw on
landing was a notice-board with the following inscription:

THE RIVER BEING DANGEROUS
BELOW THE CHURCHYARD A
BARRIER HAS BEEN PLACED
ACROSS TO PREVENT PLEASURE
BOATS FROM GOING DOWN.

    This did not alarm us very much, as we had already passed over or
15   round a considerable number of barriers of one sort or another. We
left our boat in charge of an old woman, and walked up to the Post
Office, where we got our letters: saw Shakespeare's house, which is
just opposite, then wended our way to Holy Trinity Church, Fred
causing us considerable amusement from the fact of his walking about
20   with a telegraph form which somebody had stuck to the back of his
coat. The Church is approached by an avenue of very fine trees: we
went in and were shown over the place, saw many old monuments, also
the American window, a beautiful stained glass, to which American
visitors only subscribe. It represents the seven ages of man, illustrated
25   from the Bible. The verger called our attention to some exceedingly
quaint carvings in oak on the choir-stalls. They were very funny, I
will not explain the subjects, but certainly advise anyone who goes
there to examine them. They will find it well worth the trouble. The
lectern and chancel rails were covered up with drapery, but the verger
30   uncovered them; they were very beautiful, all of decorated brass,
inlaid with stones. We saw Shakespeare's bust in a niche in the wall
inside the communion rails just above the place where he was buried.

There is a stone slab over his grave, with the following inscription
engraved on it:-

GOOD FRIEND FOR JESUS SAKE FORBEARE
TO DIGG THE DUST ENCLOASED HEARE
BLESTE BE YE MAN YT SPARES THE STONES   5
AND CURSTE BE HE YT MOVES MY BONES.

After leaving the church, we strolled through the town, and
returned to the place where we had left the boat. We then remembered
we had no bread for lunch, so Fred and I started off to get some. We
went in to four shops but it was all stale. Fred swore at me for wasting   10
so much time, but I did not see the force of being compelled to eat
stale bread with our cheese and butter. We got some new loaves at last,
and rejoined the others. We started at 1.30 and after passing the
churchyard we were brought to a stop by a very old and delapidated
lock, the gates of which were full of holes, and to which there were no   15
windlasses. We could see no other barrier, so presumed the barrier
referred to on the notice board must be the lock. This was certainly a
very formidable barrier, as on landing, and examining the ground we
found things in a very bad position. The bank below the lock was

about 10 feet high for about 50 yards, and then came a little stream
which ran into the river at right angles down a deep gully, the sides of
which were thick mud and covered with bushes. There was a single
plank foot-bridge across this, but it was too far across, and altogether
5   too narrow and shaky for us to think of carrying the boat across it. On
the side of the bridge was a semicircular excavation leading down to
the stream with a drop from the field of about four feet. It was where
the drainage of the field ran into the stream, and to make matters
worse, there was in the middle of this a number of large jagged stones,
10   which would certainly have damaged the bottom of the boat if it had
come in contact with them. We put our heads together, and consulted
what was best to be done, and arrived at the conclusion that the only
feasible plan was to get the boat down in the gully and push it into the
river. Fortunately we saw some hurdles in the field, so we quickly
15   collected some, and laid them down over the mud and stones, making
a sort of pathway with them down to the bottom of the gully. We then
got the boat out of the water, took everything out, and with the help of
the rollers got the bow onto the first hurdle. We then lifted it forward

and got the stern on, and gradually edged it inch by inch to the
bottom. We were very cramped for room in doing this, as there was a
nasty shoulder of high bank round which we had to screw the boat.
When we got it safely to the bottom we had to wade through the mud
and keep it moving towards the river, much inconvenienced all the   5
time by the thick bushes. It took us a long time, even after this. Two
of us held the boat's bow up from the top of the bank by the painter,

whilst the other three worked at the stern, and at last we had the
satisfaction of seeing it float out of the entrance of the gully. I sculled
round to the high bank, and we put everything back into its place, not
forgetting the hurdles, which had served us a very good turn. This
little job had occupied us three quarters of an hour, so we immediately
got out our lunch, and consumed it on the side of the lock. We got
away again at 2.30, sculled for 3 miles, and arrived at Lower
Millcote, where there was a lock. This looked in such bad condition
that we thought to save time it would be better to carry the boat round
at once, but just then two old men arrived upon the scene, and after a
deal of patching with sluice-boards, they got one gate a little way open,
through which we squeezed. We gave them something for their
trouble, and sculled on past Welford, and round a bend of the river to
the Mill. Here there was a lock and a weir in one line stretching
completely across our path: we saw an old man and his daughter in a
punt full of witheys in the lock, so we hailed them, and the man
opened the gates for us. He said he was the "Wyre Setter", and he
gave us a deal of information about the river below. We went on for

two miles further to Grange Mill, where there was another lock. This
compared rather favourably with the condition of the others, as far as
appearance went, so we expected to get through with little or no
trouble, but its looks were very deceptive, for when we got in, we
found the water ran out of the lower gates as fast as it came in at the

upper ones. We waited patiently for some time, but found that the
water kept the same level, so we had to shut the bottom sluices and go
out again. We hauled the boat out onto the bank, and rolled it across a
field for about 100 yards to where there was a shelving bank, where
we launched it. We heard afterwards that this lock had been damaged   5
by the floods, but we didn't put much faith in it, as it was only like the
majority of the others on the Avon. We were getting tired with such
tremendously hard work, so were half inclined to stop at Bidford for
the night, but we saw marked on the map a small inn about 5 miles
further down, so we determined to push on, and take our chance of   10
getting beds.

At Bidford we passed through a flood-gate which was worked by a
windlass by a man on shore. We sculled on past Marl Cliff Hill, a
very lovely place, and arrived at Cleve Lock, which was also useless,
and we again had to roll the boat round a long way across a field before   15
we could find a safe place to launch it. Harvington Mill was the next

obstacle; the lock here was all in pieces, only one gate being left; the
others had fallen down, and the lock was full of large stones, which
had fallen away from the sides. This was a regular puzzler: we could
not possibly draw the boat up the right bank, as there was a high stone
5   parapet, and on the other side it was equally impracticable, as there
were thick bushes right down to the water's edge, and an orchard
behind. We landed and looked about the place, went across the
orchard and tasted the apples, and found that we could take the boat
down the weir, one side of which was dry and covered with rushes. I
10   then returned and sculled round to the other side of the orchard,
leaving the others there enjoying the fruit. We easily rolled the boat

down the weir, and sculled away, not forgetting to fill our pockets
with apples by way of a reminder of the place. At 8 o'clock we reached
the "Fish-Anchor Hotel"; it is a very small inn, situated quite by itself
15   at the top of a very steep bank. Down this bank there were some
wooden steps leading into the water, and just below there is a punt
kept to ferry passengers across. At first we did not notice the steps, and
overshot the mark, (as we could hardly see the Inn from the river, it
being so high up) and we had to turn round and row back, when we
20   immediately discovered the vast differences between going *up* and

*down*stream. We fastened the boat to the bottom of the stairs, and having ascertained that we could be accommodated at the Inn, we stripped the boat, and passed the things from one to another up the stairs. As we were putting the sculls and cushions in a stable, we heard a hail from the opposite side of the river from a man who wished to   5 come across, but as "George", who attended the ferry, had gone to bed, the man was in a fix. I therefore took a pair of sculls, and went

across and fetched him, for which he was very grateful. When we came to enquire what they could give us to eat, we were quietly informed that they had nothing in the house, but bread and butter. As we thought this would hardly be substantial enough for us after our
5   hard day's work, we impressed upon the landlord the advisability of fetching something. He informed us that the nearest village was Offenham, three miles off, but we soon saw him start off with a basket on his arm to walk there, and buy what he could find. Meanwhile we walked about the place, and chatted to some men who had been fishing
10   and were returning home. Clarke was very much interested to see them put away a quart of very sour beer while they were sitting outside the house. Our host returned at 9.30 with the grub, and we sat down to it a little before 10. Again it was eggs and bacon; the bacon was very hard, and the lamp smelt horribly, but we were so awfully hungry that
15   we hardly thought of the discomforts until we had finished. There were only two beds at our disposal, and one of these belonged to the good man and his wife, so where they slept Goodness only knows. Fortunately there was a sofa in the parlour; we tossed for this and Tom won it. George and Clarke had already had one taste of sofa, so they
20   were exempt from tossing. Fred and I occupied one bed, and George and Clarke the other. After supper we went out for a stroll, and George was suddenly taken queer which we attributed to the green apples he had so freely partaken of. In this case the "Stolen fruit turned out to be anything but sweet", as George very soon found out,
25   however, we gave him some brandy and he soon recovered.

Thursday, August 5th

Fred and I got up at 6, went down the steps, and took the boat down to the beach where the ferry punt lay, hauled it up, baled it out, and cleaned it. We put the stores in and got the boat ready for starting. We caught a donkey, and I had a ride, but it was a very small one, as my feet touched the ground. We went in to breakfast at 7, and had the remnants of last night's feast, that is to say, more ham and eggs. The ham was, if possible, harder than what we had had the night before, and the bread was frightfully stale, in fact, everything about the place was very ancient. We thought at least that in an antedeluvian place like that we should get off with a very small bill, and thus balm our wounded feelings, but when it was presented to us, we found that we had to pay quite as much, if not more, than we usually did at other places, where we fared very much better. However, it was better than if we had gone on the night before after dark, as there was no knowing what damage we might have done ourselves, being in strange water, and there being so many difficulties to overcome. We got away at 8.15, and after sculling half a mile we were stopped by a lock that was all in pieces. We rolled the boat about 150 yards, and launched it down a gully without much difficulty. Tom and I sculled to Evesham, and just before we got to the town we came to a lock; the gates were all standing, but had enormous holes in them, through which the water rushed in cascades. Of course it was useless attempting to get through, and as we found part of the weir was dry, we rolled the boat down without taking the luggage out, there being a capital incline. At Evesham there happened to be a Regatta and flower show; we should have liked to have stopped there, and seen what it was like, but if we had done so, we should not have been able to arrive at Hereford on Saturday, and we wanted to spend Sunday there. The town was gaily decorated and we saw lots of girls busy arranging the flowers in the tents. As we went along below the town, we passed a four-oared racing

boat coming up-stream. The fellows were duffers, the oars going like
the sails of a windmill, and nearly swamping themselves with the
splashing they made. Two miles past Evesham we came to a lock that
was in capital order, and had winches attached. On George and myself
5   landing we found a boat inside containing two men and two girls who
were going up to the Regatta. They informed us that they (the men,
not the girls) had had to carry their boat up a weir further down. We
passed through, and got into a long reach where the wind blew dead
against us; it was wretchedly cold, with no sun and a dull sky. At
10 Fladbury Mill, Clarke very nearly came to grief again. We had gone
through the lock, and were waiting for Fred and George to get in.
Clarke had hold of the bank with a boathook, pulling hard to keep the
boat steady in the stream, when the bank gave way, and he went head
over heels, fortunately in the boat, and not over the side. At
15 Cropthorn there was a weir and swing sluice, which opened with a
chain attached to a wheel on the bank. This required two to work it so
that was probably the reason why the people we met could not manage
it, as they could not leave the girls in the boat alone. Clarke and Tom
then sculled on, while George, Fred and I had a run for a mile along
20 the bank. After passing Wyre Piddle we saw an orchard, some of the
trees in which overhung the water. We steered under them, and
Clarke took up an oar and made a dash at a bough above; he missed it,
but nearly killed poor George who was quietly sitting in the bow, the
oar swinging down just past his head. The next shot was more
25 successful, and a shower of apples came down in and around the boat.
These we quickly picked up and demolished, altho' they were far from
sweet, but we were not particular after the miserable breakfast we had
had in the morning. We knocked some more down and stowed them
away for dessert, and then found there was a countryman quietly
30 staring at us from the orchard. He did not volunteer any remark,
neither did we, but rowed away. While we were going through Wyre
Piddle Lock we were accosted by a very loquacious farmer, who,
among other things told us that there were a great many orchards
along the banks further down. This was very good news, although at
35 first we thought he twigged our appropriation of apples.

At Pershore Bridge we landed, George and Clarke walked up into
the town about half a mile off to buy some grub, whilst Fred, Tom
and I strolled on and near the bridge smoking, we got into conversation with a blind man, who was walking towards the town. He insisted
40 on shaking hands with me, as he thought he recognised in mine, the
voice of one of his neighbours. I told him that I had not the pleasure of

being a friend of his, but it was a long time before he would believe I wasn't joking. When George and Clarke returned, we got in the boat and had lunch. We arrived at the Swing Sluice below the town at 2.30. This was very difficult to open, so awfully stiff, and as we had expended a considerable time in opening it, and as it apparently would take the same time to shut, we left it as it was, rightly thinking that someone would soon close it, and sure enough, we had only gone a short distance when a man rushed along the bank gesticulating and shouting most wildly, probably with the hope of inducing us to come back. This we hardly cared about doing, and we had the satisfaction of seeing him shut it himself. We pulled up at an orchard near Birlington Lock, but did not land, as the apples looked too sour, even for us, you see we had learnt experience, at least George had. Nearly the whole of the day we had seen Bredon Hill, which is very high: the river ran round nearly three sides of it. This hill we kept in sight until we arrived at Tewkesbury. At Stafford Mill we did not land, as two millers volunteered to open the lock for us. We passed through, and

George had got some money out to give them, when the stream carried
us rapidly down the river, and so the poor fellows lost their gratuity.
They did not say anything, but looked awfully sold and indeed it was
hard upon them, but what could we do? Soon after this we passed
5   under Eckington Railway Bridge, very finely constructed of open
ironwork. At Eckington Mill we again came across more effects of the

floods, as there, a large bridge had been completely carried away, and
we could see that the water had risen to the first floor windows. After
this, I being very sleepy, lay down in the bow, wrapped myself up and
10   went to sleep, and did not wake until we very nearly reached
Tewkesbury. We arrived at that town at 6: our route then lay down
the Severn, and we had to pass through a lock from one river to the
other. We went underneath a very queer old stone bridge, and passed
a number of wharves and factories. When we got to the lock, we

found some lighters going through, and as we did not care about waiting, we turned back and landed at the Boathouse, where we left the boat for the night with instructions for it to be ready for us by 9 o'clock the next morning. We were recommended to go to the Swan Hotel, as being the best in the place, and we accordingly walked along the principal street for a considerable distance, until we reached it. Our impression of the town was anything but lively. The shops were all closed, as if it were Sunday, and those few people that were about, stared at us as if we had been wild beasts. On arriving at the hotel we ordered supper, changed our things, wrote some letters and then went out for a stroll and to see the Abbey, the only place of interest in the town, I believe, and this did not prove particularly interesting to us, as it was locked up for the day, and the outside was certainly not beautiful. We were much struck with the melancholy appearance of the town, on enquiry we heard that nearly all the shops shut at 5 p.m. on Thursday, so we were unfortunate in our day.

It is altogether a very queer old place, and looked as if it had been built in the year 1: the houses are very antedeluvian and irregular, hardly two alike, and the shops (at least those that were open) were very small and insignificant. One, I noticed, was marked over the door "Fruiterer" and inside the place was full of old clothes, and at a toy-shop, tea and coffee were dispensed behind the counter. We had supper at 8, and were much amused at the waitress, who, after we had sent her for something, begged us to make up our minds all at once what we wanted, and she would fetch the lot altogether, as she didn't like running up and down stairs so often. We replied that we could not measure off our appetites to a crumb, and of course as we finished the chops, the milk, and the butter etc at different times, and almost invariably required a fresh supply, it was hardly to be expected we could comply with her polite request. After tea we sat out on the balcony and smoked, and watched the volatilities of some young dressmakers through an open window in the opposite house. When it was dark, we took a walk into the country at the back of the town, and returned to bed at 10. George, Tom and Clarke had a double-bedded room, whilst Fred and I slept together.

Memo: When you go to Tewkesbury, don't stop at the Swan Hotel, the place is dirty, the attendance is inefficient and the charges are very stiff.

Friday, August 6th

We got up at 7, and found it drizzling with rain. Had breakfast at
8, cold beef and eggs, and then went out again to see the Abbey, but as
it did not open until 10, we would not wait. George, Tom and I went
down to the boathouse, and found everything in readiness for us, for
5   the men had carried the boat through the yard, and launched it in a
back-water leading to the Severn, so that we should not have to go
through the river lock. The boathouse was a very large one, and
contained a number of racing and wager boats belonging to various
clubs. Fred and Clarke having arrived, we started away at 9.15. We
10   sculled down the backwater, and soon found ourselves in the Severn.
We soon heard a sound of falling water, and proceeding very
cautiously, we distinguished right ahead of us a mark across the river,
which on our nearer approach, we found to be a weir with a heavy fall.
There was no notice board or post to mark it, and nothing to let one
15   know of its being there, except the sound of the fall, so that if we had
come there at night, we should probably have gone over it. We saw a
bend in the river on one side of the weir, so turned round there, and
came in view of an immense lock. large enough to admit a ship or
steamer passing through. One gate was open, so after hailing the
20   keeper, we went in, and lay on our sculls in the middle. I had never
been in such an enormous lock before; the walls were quite 30 feet
high, and all we had to do was to keep our sculls in the water, and
steady the boat. The lock-keeper shut us in, and by means of hydraulic
machinery let the water out. The fall was only about five feet; there
25   was nothing to pay. On emerging into the river, we had a full view of
the weir, and we congratulated ourselves on not having gone over it,
as it looked very formidable. The Severn at this part, and in fact, all
the way to Gloucester is very wide, and the stream very sluggish.
There is no scenery to speak of; the surrounding country is very flat,
30   and on each side of the river there are high banks, so that we could

really see nothing. As we passed Deerhurst, we came across some men fishing from boats with nets that stretched right across the river. When passing under Haw Bridge, we very nearly ran foul of a sunken barge, we only just managed to get out of the way; it was just covered with water, so that we could not see it until we were close by, and if we had run on it, we should in all probability have sunk, as we were going at a good pace. Soon afterwards we saw a lovely public house (the Red Lion) on the left bank, and determined to get out and get something to drink. It was situated at a bend of the river where there was a very shallow landing place. The ground being red earthy clay, it was some little time before we could punt the boat sufficiently near to effect a landing. We then all got out and went into the public house, and tasted the cider and perry, but we none of us seemed to care about either, so we filled a can with beer. There was an orchard close by the house, so I fetched a boathook and tried to get some apples from the opposite side of the hedge, but tall as I am, I could not manage it, so we returned to the boat disappointed. I was the next one to come to grief; Clarke wanted a rush to clean his pipe with, so I steered close to the bank, and as we went past, caught hold of a handful, but they would not easily break and slipped out of my hand, cutting my first finger completely round, and very deep. I bound it up as well as I could, but it quite incapacitated me from sculling for the time. The others landed me, and I took a constitutional along the bank for two or three miles. From the tow-path of course I could see the country, and very wet it looked from the floods. The water must have risen to an immense height to have flowed over the banks, but as all the land on the other side was much below their level, it had inundated the country for miles round, and the fields, orchards and gardens were still several feet deep with water. In some brick fields and kilns, I noticed men hard at work pumping the water back into the river. We saw on the map that a branch of the river about a mile above Gloucester led direct to Over, where we had to get into the Hereford-Gloucester canal, and we, of course, intended going along this branch, but some men I spoke to told me that there were several weirs in it, and no locks, so that we could not go that way, but would have to follow the mainstream, go through Gloucester, and round Alney Island to Over. These men either knew nothing at all about it, or else were most abominable liars, for the lock-keeper at Over afterwards told us that the branch was quite clear, and was the usual route for barges. I hailed the boat, told them what I had heard, and climbed down the bank into a barge that some men were unloading, and the

others took me into the boat. We very soon after this approached
Gloucester. We hurried past some most offensive chemical works, and
a good deal of small shipping, and went under a large iron Tubular
Railway Bridge, which is so constructed that it swings round on a
5   pivot in the centre, to allow vessels to pass. The water here was very
dirty, and the streets that ran alongside the river, equally so. We were
very glad to get out of it, and round the bend, through a lock to Over.
Here we went into a deep lock which leads to the canal. Fred and I
climbed up the wall, and went into the lock-house, while the other
10   three took the boat through. I asked for our pass and the man made it
out for me, and wanted to charge 15/-, but fortunately I had a letter
with me which I had received in London from the Canal Company
stating that the charge would be 10/-; this I triumphantly produced, so
the man was done out of his expected bonus. We made the boat fast
15   behind some barges outside the lock, and telling the keeper we should
be back in an hour or two, we started to walk to Gloucester, which was
on the other side of the river, about a mile distant. On the road I
managed to reach some apples over a hedge, but we could not eat
them, they were so sour. As we were going over the bridge it began to
20   rain heavily. We had left our macintoshes in the boat, but did not
think it worthwhile to go back for them, so we turned up our coat
collars, and hurried on. Tom, Fred and I walked up a long street to
the Post Office, and got the letters, promising to meet George and
Clarke at the Cathedral. On our way back we went into a confectioner's
25   shop and ate heaps of things that were not good for us, then went on to
George and Clarke, who were patiently waiting for us at the door of
the Cathedral. We all went in, and putting ourselves under the
guardianship of a verger, were shown over the place. It is very
beautiful, and to my mind infinitely more grand and imposing than
30   most of the churches and cathedrals I have seen on the continent.
There are many fine old monuments, one is the tomb of one of
William the Conqueror's sons, with a carved wooden effigy of him, in
perfect preservation. There are many little chapels round the sides of
the Cathedral; one of these has no walls at all, but is almost entirely
35   built of stained glass, with light stone pillars as support to the roof.
Another chapel dedicated to St. Andrew has the walls covered with
beautiful frescoes, all painted by an amateur artist of the neighbourhood. It took him three or four years to complete and was only just
finished. We went up a little winding stone staircase leading to a stone
40   gallery, where formerly the choir used to sing. The Reredos is new
and very beautiful. After having seen the whole of the interior, we

were shown through the cloisters, and then went down in the crypt, where there were several more small chapels, and a very ancient stone altar.

After leaving the Cathedral, we bought some bread, and returned to Over. It was still raining, so I put on my macintosh and sou'wester, took the tow-line, and we commenced our journey along the Hereford-Gloucester Canal, which leads to, and terminates at Hereford. We could not think of sculling at first, as the rushes covered the whole of the water, with the exception of about six feet in the middle, just space enough to allow a barge to go along. From the tow-path I could see nothing of the boat, the reeds and rushes standing from 6 to 8 feet high. The rain fortunately soon ceased, and we got out the grub. We were in a hurry, so I ate my lunch as I towed, while the others had their's in the boat. The scenery for the first five miles was really beautiful; I have rarely seen finer anywhere. We would occasionally see between the trees lovely little glimpses of the Severn Valley far away down on our right, backed by a range of hills; but what we most admired was the wood through which we were passing. The trees on either side hung down sometimes drooping into the water, and others meeting and forming a perfect canopy above our heads, almost shutting out the light. Ferns and wild flowers were growing down to the water's edge: there was not a living soul or a habitation to be seen, and not a sound to be heard except the singing of the birds. Altogether the place was most beautiful, and we were very sorry when we presently emerged from the wood.

At the first lock I gave up the tow-line, and while the others were getting the boat through, I took a can and made my way to a farmhouse that I saw some little distance off. I asked the good man of the house whether he would sell me any milk, but he refused, saying they wanted all they had; but his wife having come in, I used my eloquence on her, and after a good deal of persuasion she gave me a quart, and as much as I liked to drink, on the premises, of which latter offer, too, I took advantage, as I was very thirsty after my long walk. We found our winch rather small for the locks on this canal, so one of the keepers kindly gave us a larger one in exchange. About 4.30 it came on to pour with rain again, and we waited under a bridge for some time and consulted as to where we should pass the night. We had intended to have gone on to Dymock, but as we had lost a good deal of time at Gloucester, and also had not made a very early start in the morning, we decided on stopping at Newent. After having arrived at this decision, we left our shelter, and very soon came to what we found

to be a most extraordinary double lock. It was an immense thing with about 30 feet fall, and a pair of gates in the middle. None of us had ever come across such an affair as this before, and we had no idea how to manage it; there was not a soul to be seen, so we could get no

5   information on the subject. We took the boat in, shut the rear gates, and let down the sluices; then opened the middle gates, and let in the water at the top sluices, but by some extraordinary means, the water, as soon as it came in, rushed out again through some invisible exit, and as there was a ledge across the middle of the lock, we could not get

10   sufficient in to float over. We experimentized there for over half an hour; at last we made a tremendous effort, and having let the water in with a rush, by means of pulling with boat-hooks and lugging at the sides, we managed to get over the ledge, and float in the upper half of the lock. Our difficulty then was over, for we had only to shut the

15   middle gates, when the upper half soon filled, and we easily went through. This was the only lock of its kind that we came across during our tour, and to this day I have no idea how it is worked. We went through four or five more locks and shortly before reaching Newent

the rain ceased, and it came out fine. Newent is a small town, with a straggling street, nearly a mile long. We landed at a wharf close beside the bridge, on which a large crowd soon assembled to see us disembark. We locked all the moveables up in a barn which the proprietor of the wharf kindly placed at our disposal, and gave the boat in charge of some bargees who had their craft moored alongside. A mile beyond Newent there is a tunnel nearly two miles long, which we had to go through; we made enquiries of the bargees about the hours of going through, and they told us that craft going in the direction of Hereford would have to go through between the hours of 6 and 9, and 12 and 3, both fore and afternoon. They further informed us that they were going to take a barge through the following morning, and said we could tow behind them and get through that way without trouble. We did not much like the idea, as a barge takes nearly three hours to get through, but they so evidently thought that the best plan, that we said nothing more about it, but waited for what the morning would bring forth. We shouldered our luggage, and walked up the street to the Red Lion; on enquiry we found that they had only one bed, and thinking that hardly sufficient for five, we continued our walk until we arrived at the "George Inn",

5
10
15
20

"For what we are about to receive"

where we found a jolly old landlady, a very nice daughter, and capital rooms. We had some chops for supper at 8.45, and everything was served up very nicely. Whilst feeding we were visited by a beautiful

Newfoundland dog, who appeared to swallow the chop bones whole, and who was altogether a remarkable animal, for when I gave him a halfpenny he immediately went out and bought himself a biscuit. We wrote some letters after supper, and went out and posted them. We strolled about and smoked, but it was so pitch dark that we were afraid to go far. At 9.30 there was not a single light in the streets that we could see, except that in our own room. The inhabitants of Newent are evidently early birds, everybody appeared to be in bed, so we very soon followed their example. Fred and I slept together, George and Tom also slept together, and Clarke had the luxury of a room to himself, in fact, we generally managed that he should have this luxury, when possible, as he snored and ground his teeth so fearfully, that we all preferred being some distance from him at night.

Saturday, August 7th

We got up at 5.30, and had breakfast at 6. The old lady of the house was awfully kind; she made not the slightest bother about our wanting a meal so early, but had some hot chops prepared, and got up herself to see that we were comfortable. Before the others had finished, I went down to the wharf, got the key of the barn, and with plenty of willing 5
hands to assist me, I soon got the boat ready. The other four shortly turned up, but we found we had left the rug behind at the Inn, so George walked back to fetch it, and then came along the tow-path, and caught us up at the second lock. We passed through four locks, and then met the bargees to whom we had spoken the night before. They 10
told us they had orders not to proceed along the canal, so we should not be able to get through the tunnel with them, which information we received with joy, as we wished to go through alone, fully expecting to get through in an hour at the outside. The tunnel had not a very inviting aspect; it was very small and narrow, and looked more like a 15
sewer than anything else; it was so small that two craft going in opposite directions could not pass each other. That is the reason why there were specific times for going through. The bargees lie on their backs on the top of their barge, and push along the roof with their hands and feet. We lit our lamp, and entered at 7.25. George and 20
Clarke sat in the stern, Tom and Fred pushed along on either side with boathooks, and I knelt in the bow with the lamp. Very soon after we had got in, the tunnel made a turn, and we could see neither one end or the other, and were in complete darkness, with the exception of the glimmer from the lantern, which only made the darkness visible. 25
It was a melancholy sort of place, not calculated to put one in the liveliest spirits, so I started a song, which revived us all, and we sang part-songs and choruses all the way through. It sounded very well too, echoing and reverberating along the tunnel. We were suddenly stopped by a shout from Fred, who said he had dropped his boathook. 30

We pushed back a little way, and I passed the lamp aft and after much groping about we found it. Fortunately it was the paddle boathook, as it floated well. As we were near the middle, I thought I heard a sound ahead, and having obtained silence, we distinctly heard the sound of
5   falling water. At first we could not make out what it could be, but we soon found out that there was quite a stream of water coming through the roof. When we got close, Fred and Tom gave some vigorous pushes and we got past as quickly as possible, but we could not escape it, and found afterwards that our flannels were awfully dirty from it,
10   with many red spots, the water evidently trickled through the sandstone in the roof. We came under several more of these miniature waterfalls, and got out of the other end at 8, having been just 35 minutes inside, which I consider not bad work for novices at that sort of game.

Outside the tunnel the banks were again very beautiful, similar to the first five miles of the canal. Tom and George attempted to scull here, but the canal was so narrow, and the water so covered with rushes, that they soon gave up, and Tom took the towline, whilst Clarke went ahead, and opened the gates and locks. Clarke was followed for some distance by a drove of little pigs. There must have been something peculiar about him to attract pigs in the way he did; once before at Heyford a similar thing happened. Even if the water had allowed, I should have been unable to scull, as my finger was still very painful, although the old lady at the "George" had bound it up for me with some special plaster of her own. It was a fearfully dull and miserable day, a damp mist falling and occasionally rain. We passed through seven locks before we reached Ledbury; there we landed, leaving the boat in charge of a lockman. It was raining at the time, so we walked up the town in full wet-weather costume, macintoshes, leggings, and sou'westers, and carrying the cans in our hands. The people rushed

out to the shop-doors to look at us, and no doubt we did present a very curious appearance. Ledbury is a good sized town, plenty of life and bustle, but some of the houses looked very antiquated. We walked up to the church, but it was locked. Clarke and I smoked in the churchyard, while the other three went to look at the prospect. When

they returned, we went back into the principal street, bought some
beer and bread, and very much astonished the proprietor and the
customers of a large grocer's shop, by all trooping in, and asking for
half a pound of butter. They let us have this, and we went to several
5 places to try and get some milk; but we were unsuccessful. We saw a
coach pull up at an Hotel to change horses, with a lot of ladies on the
top, who stared at us as if we were savages. This coach came from Ross;
it runs three times a week. We stopped at Ledbury about an hour, then
went back to the lock where we had left our boat, and which we found
10 surrounded by a swarm of little children. We sculled on for about half
a mile, hoping they would disperse, but about half a dozen of the dirty
little enthusiasts were evidently bent on seeing us eat our lunch, for
they would not go away, notwithstanding the most awful threats. We
pulled up under a bridge for lunch, and as they still hovered about,
15 George made a rush after them. He caught one, and held him over the
water, threatening to drop him in unless he made off with his
companions. We had lunch, and went on again at 1.30, and it then
began to rain again, and it kept off and on in showers all the rest of the
day. From Ledbury we had a ten mile pound, and we took it in turns
20 to tow, sculling being out of the question. We went through another
tunnel about 400 yards long; Fred was towing at the time, and as there
was a tow-path through it, we suggested he should tow us through.
This he attempted to do, but he very soon begged us to let him in, as
the path was about half a foot thick in mud and slush. We therefore
25 pushed through with boathooks. We did not light the lamp, as we
could see daylight at the other end. We went through three very deep
locks, and another tunnel about a quarter of a mile long. We tried to
light the lamp, but the oil bottle had been mislaid; as we pushed into
the darkness, however, we soon came to a curve, and saw the light at
30 the other end, and we got through without mishap. We made two
raids on orchards, but the result was hardly worth the trouble, as the
apples were very green. We arrived at Hereford about dusk, and
pulled up at a timber wharf. Fred and I landed, and walked through
the city to the old Wye Bridge, calling on the way for letters. On the
35 bridge we found young Jordan, son of the boathouse proprietor, and
we explained to him what we wanted. We went to the boathouse, got a
truck and two men and returned to the wharf, where we found the
others patiently waiting in the drizzling rain. With the assistance of
the two men, we pulled the boat out of the water, and placed it on the
40 truck; we then replaced all the things in the boat, and started throuth
the city. It was now dark, but being Saturday, the shops were all

lighted up, and there were heaps of people about the place who stared at us in amazement, as with our macintoshes and sou'westers, we resembled dustmen more than anything else. We had been recommented to stay at the "City Arms Hotel", so as we passed there, we stopped the truck, took out the baggage, and let the men go on with   5
the boat to the boathouse, Jordan having met us at the hotel. We were very glad to get to our rooms, and have a change and wash. We came down to supper at 9, steak and eggs. Afterwards we went into the bar parlour, smoked and had some grog. We went to bed at 11, Fred and I in a double bedded room, Tom and George in another, and Clarke   10
by himself.

Sunday, August 8th

We were pretty tired out with our previous day's hard work, and as we intended to make this a complete day's rest, we did not get up until 9.30. It was a very fine sunny day, a great contrast to the day before. Had breakfast at 10, ham and eggs, found out that the
5 Cathedral service commenced at 11, and accordingly at the proper time we all trooped in. I was sitting in the end chair in the middle aisle, when I saw a friend of mine Flemming gravely walking along with some ladies. As he went past me I pinched his leg, and when he looked down he greeted me with the most utter look of astonishment.
10 He, however, was not the only one that appeared astonished. Other people stared, and probably wondered what we were, and, no doubt, our appearance quite justified their wondering. Five great tall fellows, tanned as red as Indians, with no prayer-books, and their costumes anything but suitable for church. The Cathedral had nothing particu-
15 larly striking inside, except the choir screen which is very beautiful, as also is the chancel. After the service was over, George, Tom and I walked with Flemming to the place where he was staying, and when we left him, we cut across some fields, and came to the river. We followed its windings for over a mile, then returned to the Hotel.
20 Had a capital dinner at 2.30, roast lamb, apple pudding, plum pudding etc. We stopped in for a short time to allow this to digest, as it was the first meal of its kind we had had since we started. We wrote some letters, then Fred, Tom and I walked down to the boathouse, and had a long chat with Jordan and his son, who were both very civil
25 and obliging fellows. Among other items of information they gave us, one that rather staggered us, for they said that the steamer which used to sail daily from Chepstow to Bristol had been sunk through collision, and the owners had not started another one. It was by means of this steamer we anticipated getting across the mouth of the Severn.
30 Jordan said that in fine weather, one might easily pull across the whole

way, but at any rate, if we put ourselves under the guardianship of Mr James at Chepstow, he would tell us what would be best to be done. We started along the river bank for about half a mile, then lay down on the grass and smoked, Fred and Tom got out their sketching materials, and having failed in inveigling some rustic damsels to sit, sketched each other in various attitudes. In the meantime, George and Clarke had gone for a long walk to some Gas Works, where there was a very fine view. We went back at 7.30, and hung out of the windows of our sitting room watching the people come from church. Had tea at 8.30, bread and butter and eggs, then all went to the bar parlour, where we smoked and grogged until 11. Fred apparently wished to have his grog for nothing, as he was quietly stealing off to bed, but was smartly collared by the old lady who was attending to us, and who made him pay for it.

Monday, August 9th

We got up at 7.30, and packed our things, which had been all dried after the wetting they got on Saturday. Had breakfast at 8, chops and eggs, and then walked off in detachments to the river. I did some shopping on the road, purchasing a "Sailor's Friend", price 9*d*, and a large sheet of sticking plaster, price 1*d*. This was for binding up my wounded finger, but I very much regretted afterwards that I had been foolish enough to buy it, for although inexpensive, it was decidedly adhesive, and not only could I not get the piece off my finger when it was once on, but the rest of the sheet, which I had put in my pocket as a reserve, glued it together as entirely as if it had been sewn up. I passed a photograph shop on my way to the river, and, of course, on looking inside, I found Fred there, turning the views over by scores. If there was a photographer's shop in any place we passed through, Fred was sure to find it out. I went in, and tried to get him to come away, but he hadn't decided on what he wanted, so I went down to the boathouse where the others were waiting. Fred shortly appeared, and we started away at 9.15, after receiving a good many useful hints from Jordan, as to the best course to pursue.

Tom and I started off sculling, and Clarke steered, and we immediately shot the second arch of the bridge, on which a good many people had assembled to see us start. The River Wye is something after the same style as the Avon, although much larger. It is very shallow in many places, and the stream is very rapid. The river is not locked at all; there are many falls, which are called streams. These are really natural weirs, over which the water rushes with great velocity, and it is only by keeping one's boat well away from the breakers, that one can ensure going down without a spill. About two miles above Ox Ford we came to a very nasty stream at a bend of the river: this being the first, we did not know exactly how to manage, and Clarke thinking the best plan would be to go slap through it, ran us aground. We all

jumped out except Clarke, and held the boat steady, while we gently and cautiously pushed it into deep water. We jumped in again, but before Tom and I had got our sculls out, Clarke uttered a yell, and we found we were being carried by the stream straight on to an enormous snag, sticking up out of the water. The rudder was quite useless, as the stream was powerful, Tom and I however, quickly got out our bow sculls, and giving one or two tremendous heaves, we just managed to clear it. Shortly after this we saw a farmhouse on the bank, so Tom and I landed, and went in, and asked the mistress to sell us some milk. While there a heavy rain shower came on, so we stayed in the house and chatted to the old woman, the other three preferring the boat. Whilst waiting for the milk, I was larking about with an axe and block, when the former flew off the latter, and caught me on the leg. Fortunately the axe was awfully blunt, as it only just cut the skin: as my legs were bare at the time, it was a fortunate escape. We got a gallon of milk, and continued our course, looking out for a place where we could buy something to eat. At a little place called Hoarwithy, Tom and I went ashore. We walked into the village, and found there were two rival shops. We gave them each a turn, buying bread at one, and a pot of marmalade at the other. We returned, and lunched in the boat. Just after we started again, we passed under a very

dilapidated old wooden bridge, the two side arches were propped up, but in the centre it had a tremendous drop, which made it appear very unsafe, although we were told that loads of grain sometimes went across without accident. Soon afterwards I heard a great noise on the
5   bank, and caught sight of a sheep which had fallen into a ditch, and could not get out again, its long wool having caught in some thorn bushes. It was surrounded by a large number of sheep, who were making a great noise as if calling attention to the misfortune of their companion. Fred and I therefore went ashore, and pulled it out of the
10 ditch, much to the delight of the whole flock.

Just below Sellack, we came to two shallow rapid streams close together. There were a lot of haymakers working in a field close by, who gesticulated, and shouted instructions to us, however, we could not make out what they said, so we pulled right through, although
15 grounding and bumping a good deal. The haymakers watched us with the greatest interest, and when we got safely through greeted us with cheers and hand clapping. At Lynedown we again got stuck in the

middle of the river; we all got out except Clarke and shoved the boat
into deep water, and I very nearly got a ducking through stepping into
a hole. The scenery between Hereford and Ross was very beautiful,
quite different to any we had previously seen — steep little hills
covered with beautiful foliage extended down to the water's edge, and   5
in other places rocky cliffs raised themselves perpendicularly from the
water. We reached Ross at 4.15, left the boat at a small boathouse, and
walked to the "Kings Head Hotel" changed our things, went to the
Post Office and took a stroll in the town. We afterwards walked up the
hill to the church, but we could not get inside, so had to be content   10
with looking in at a window from the top of a gravestone, which,
however, afforded us a capital view. We saw the tomb of Charles I,
and also two elm trees which grow in one of the pews. We had a
splendid view from the churchyard of the river and all the surrounding country. We then took a long walk through the woods onto the   15
hills, where we had another very extensive view, and saw a beautiful
sunset over the mountains. Coming back the descent was very steep, so

Tom and I made a rush for it down some ploughed fields, and very
soon reached the bottom. The others followed more soberly through
the woods. We saw several men fishing in coracles on the river. These
are little tiny boats about the shape of a tub, and the fishermen carry
them down to the water strapped on their backs, and look more like
huge snails on end than anything else. Had supper at 8.30, cold lamb
and salmon cutlets, and after taking another stroll in the town, went to
bed at 11. Fred and I slept together, the other three had a double-
bedded room.

Tuesday, August 10th

Got up at 7.30, and had breakfast at 8.30, chops. It began to rain while we were at breakfast, so we put off starting for a little while, in the hope of its clearing off. In the meantime we opened the windows, which looked on to the street, and attracted about a dozen dogs, making them scramble for the chop bones. It was hardly orthodox perhaps, but the dogs enjoyed it. We went down to the boat at 9.30, and found the river running like a mill sluice. In consequence of the rain it had risen five feet since the day before. We started off at a rattling pace, but had a regular gale of wind dead against us the whole day. About five miles below Ross we passed Goodrich Court, an

immense battlemented mansion belonging to a Mr Moffat, who gave £80,000 for it. It is situated on the top of beautifully wooded eminence and has large parks and grounds all round it. On a hill a little further down were the ruins of Goodrich Castle. At Welsh

 5   Bicknor we passed the body of a horse floating down stream. We saw near the river what appeared to be a large farmhouse, so George and I landed, took a can, and enquired of the mistress whether she would sell us any milk. She put more than half a gallon in the can, and said she did not sell her milk, but we were very welcome to it. We then

10   approached Symonds Yat, which is a headland which rises almost perpendicularly to a great height out of the water, and stretches across a little narrow peninsular to the river on the other side. The distance by land is 400 yards, whilst by water it is four miles. About this part is considered the finest scenery on the Wye. We rowed round this four

15   mile bend which encircles Symonds Yat, and at 12 o'clock arrived at Whitchurch or the Washings as it is called. It was then raining hard, as indeed it had been all the morning, so we thought we would land at the Ferry Inn, dry our things, have lunch, and go on to Monmouth in the afternoon. We therefore went ashore, and had some bread and

cider. The Inn was so wonderfully comfortable and outside it looked
so very much the reverse, that we unanimously agreed to stop there for
the night, and do the journey to Chepstow the next day. We therefore
told the landlady to make arrangements for our accommodation and
our dinner, and we hauled the boat up and housed it in a shed. We   5
stayed indoors smoking, reading, and sleeping, until 4.30, when the
weather having cleared up, we crossed the river by the ferry and
ascended Symonds Yat. The path was very rough and circuitous, so
when we were half-way up, Tom, Fred and I thought we would climb
to the top. We scrambled and shoved each other up, but when we   10

thought we had arrived at the top, we found we were in a deserted garden, and a considerable distance from our destination. We scrambled down again through a tall hedge, and went up by the proper path. When we arrived at the top, (which was a small bare piece of rock) we were well rewarded by a most magnificent view. We could see the river at five different places. On one side, almost directly beneath us was the water we had in the morning gone over: in front, past the bend the country was flat, so that we could see for miles and miles; a little to our left was a long range of hills far away in the background, their outline only just traceable against the sky: immediately below us, on the left was the river again, with the village of Whitchurch, and the New Wear, the roaring of which was distinctly audible even from that height; above and behind the village were the cliffs and woods of the Great Doward, the face of which was studded with holes, which had been made to quarry out the sandstone. A railway tunnel ran through Symonds Yat immediately beneath where we were standing; a train happened to come along, and it was curious to see it creep into the rocks on one side, and shortly afterwards emerge on the other. We

descended by another path which brought us close by the Railway
Station, so we crossed the line, and went down to the water's edge to
inspect the New Wear, through which we should have to pass in the
morning. It was a most formidable looking obstacle. In the centre the
rocks were heaped up in such a position that it would be impossible for   5
anything to get through, and there appeared to us to be only one
practicable passage, and that had a sharp curve which might prove
very awkward. The water rushed and roared over the rocks, making a
great noise, and altogether it looked most uninviting. We sat down
outside a little inn and had some drink, then ferried over to the other   10
side and made our way up the Great Doward, an immense rocky hill,

very steep, thickly wooded, and traversed by several narrow paths,
which intersected each other in a most perplexing manner. We saw a
cave a little way up, which had a wooden bar place across the mouth;
thinking that perhaps it was the hermit's cave, which we were in   15
search of, Fred got inside. It was very dark, so we lit some paper and
threw it in. Then we discovered it was only the entrance to a sandstone
quarry, of which there are a great many in the neighbourhood. We

wandered about on the top of the hill, but could see no hermit or his cave, so I "struck" and said I would sit down and wait for the others. I therefore selected a nice secluded spot, and having filled my pockets with wild nuts, and apples from an orchard close by, settled myself
5   down to wait. I smoked and waited and slept until it was getting dark, and as I could see nothing of the others, I went back to the Inn and watched the progress of the dinner. The others returned at 7.30, and

told me they had found "Old Sleeping Jemmy," as he was called, in a hole of a rock, about four feet square, walled round with stones and
10   turf, and roofed in with sticks; there was nothing in the shape of furniture inside. He came out to meet them, and showed them his grotto which consisted of some specimens of quartz, iron-stone etc, obtained from the mines. These were all arranged in a winding pathway among some thick bushes, though many of these were
15   enormously heavy, he declared he had carried them all there himself. This was corroborated by our landlord, who said that he was a man of remarkable strength, and told us several stories about his powers. He was a short man, with round shoulders, long hair and beard, and in consequence of his never washing himself, his skin was copper
20   coloured. He was 53 years old, and had lived 33 years in the cave.

We had dinner at 7.30, a splendid salmon, only caught a few hours before. Went to bed at 11, Fred and I slept together, George and Tom in another room, and Clarke by himself.

Wednesday, August 11th

Got up at 8, had breakfast at 8.30, cold salmon and eggs. Ballinger, our landlord, had baled and cleaned the boat, while we had been breakfasting, so we carried it down to the water, and loaded it, starting away at 9.30. It was a dull morning, and almost immediately after we started we had a shower of rain, but the wind was not so 5 violent as on the previous day. We very soon came to the New Wear, which we had taken observations of the previous afternoon. This was the longest stream we had yet come to, and would have been very

dangerous if there had been less water, only fortunately the rocks were well covered. Ballinger, by way of parting consolation, told us that two years previously, seven fellows had attempted to go down in a boat, and the boat had been smashed, and they, of course, all had a ducking. This was not encouraging for us, but we hoped to do better. Clarke was steering, Tom and Fred were sculling, and I was in the

bow. We got away on the boat, and made a rush through the smoothest water. The boat jumped up and down as if it were on the sea and I very soon got drenched with a wave that broke all over the bow of the boat. However, that didn't hurt, and we got safely through. Following this, there were very shortly two more wears, but these did not   5
prove nearly as formidable.

At 10.30 I got out and bought a gallon of milk at a farmhouse. In less than an hour after this we arrived at Monmouth, where we landed at a boathouse in a tremendous shower of rain. We left the cushions in the boathouse to dry, and putting on our macintoshes walked into the   10
town. It was a dirty looking place and nothing to see except the old bridge over the Monnow, which is more ancient than beautiful. We went to the Post Office, then bought some bread, butter and fruit; returned to the boathouse, and embarked at 12. The ruins of Raglan Castle are not far from Monmouth, but we had no time to go and see   15
them, as we were due at Chepstow that night. Just after passing under

Monmouth Bridge, we came to four wears, which we got through
without shipping any water, but we had to be very careful, as there
were many sunken rocks. We had by this time got quite accustomed to
these wears, and could generally manage to get through them without
much difficulty, except, of course, when they were extra ugly ones.
We passed Llandogo at 1: this is a pretty little village, built on the side
of a very steep hill, which rises directly from the river; looking at it
from a distance, the houses appear to be piled one on top of another.
The hill is also densely covered with trees, through which the little
white houses, and the church peep out, which had a very pretty effect.
We went a little way past the village, and then turned our thoughts to
lunch. We could not land as the banks were so steep, so we fastened
the boat to some bushes. We were not comfortable in our mooring
place, however, for the stream ran so swiftly, and there were so many
rocks around us, that we were in constant fear of breaking adrift, and
capsizing on one of them. However, we managed to enjoy our lunch,
as, indeed, we generally did, and started off again in about half an
hour. We very nearly came to grief at Coedithel's Wear; the stream
was so swift, that the boat would not answer the helm, and we were
carried through with a rush only just escaping some ugly black rocks,
and running close in to the bank. These streams generally run in a
curve, which makes it very awkward, as when this is so, one never
knows in the slightest where one is going. We had to go down another
tremendous fall going under a railway bridge just above Little
Tintern. The waves put one quite in mind of the sea, and broke
completely over the bow of the boat. Just opposite Tintern we came to
what proved to be the most dangerous wear on the river. We could
distinguish no clear passage, and could see no rocks, although we knew
there must be plenty there, as the water was so turbid and broken. The
stream also just there ran with amazing force and rapidity; we thought
the better plan would be to go at it boldly, so Fred and Tom, who had
the sculls pulled with all their strength, and we went into it like a
racehorse. When we got to the fall, the boat made a plunge through
the seething water, and came down with a tremendous shock on a
rock. Fortunately we did not capsize, as the sculls were on the water,
and steadied the boat, but we were nearly shaken from our seats. The
boat gave another bump and a grind, and then floated off. We
immediately took it to the landing steps at the Ferry Inn, and
examined the bow, which we found very considerably damaged. The
stern was torn away for some distance below the water line, and the
whole of the nose of the boat was much bent. We bound it up as best

we could with some cord, intending to have it mended in Chepstow. It had been our object to get to Tintern in time to see the Abbey, and leave when the tide was high, so that we might get over the wears easily, as at low water they are quite impassable with any safety, as there is sometimes a clear fall of five or even six feet. Some boatmen at the landing steps told us that we ought to lose no time in starting, as the tide was even then running down, so we ran up and had a look at the Abbey, and after a very short stay, we started at 2.40. We soon came to a wear, but there were no rocks visible, and plenty of water, so we found no difficulty at all, in fact we could only distinguish it by the sudden drop and rushing of the water. Clarke and Fred soon got out the oars, (which were very seldom used) and rowed along as hard as they could, as we were afraid of the tide turning on us. We were not troubled with any more wears, but the wind chopped us very strong, and, as usual, was dead against us. In some of the long reaches the

water was extremely rough, and once or twice we were in danger of
capsizing. I, lying in the bow, came in for all the wettings, as the
water constantly broke over me. The river was very wide here. We
passed the Twelve Apostles Rocks, and the Devil's Pulpit. A railway
5   was being constructed alongside the river; the line was being laid
along the side of steep rock hills for a considerable distance above
Chepstow. As we neared this town, the tide gradually fell very low, and
on either side there appeared long ugly mud banks, which rather spoilt
the effect of the beautiful scenery. We passed Chepstow Castle, which
10   is situated on the top of a high rock overlooking the river, and went on
to the town, which we reached at 4, and pulled up at some stone steps.
George and I landed, and enquired our way to the "Wye House",
occupied by Mr James, to whom we had been recommended by
Jordan at Hereford. We found him at the Inn, a stout apoplectic
15   looking old gentleman, and we forthwith engaged accommodation for
the night. We then returned to the stairs and helped to unload the
boat, after which we carried it into a workshop belonging to Mr
James, and left it there to be repaired during the night. We explained
to the old gentleman that we wanted to get across to Bristol, and asked
20   him whether we could manage it ourselves, to which he replied that it
would be madness to attempt it, and that we must be towed across. He
then fetched two boatmen, and we arranged that they should pull us
across to the mouth of the Avon on the following morning for 30/-.
They said we should have to be ready at 5 o'clock so as to start with the
25   tide. We promised we would, and then went in and washed and
changed our flannels. We ordered supper for 8 o'clock, and Clarke,
Fred and I walked up to the Post Office, and got the letters. We saw a
wedding party on the road, some of the members of which appeared
uncommonly lively. It had turned out a beautiful afternoon, so we had
30   agreed to go and see the ruins of the Castle. After we read our letters,
therefore, Fred, Clarke and I, walked up the hill and found Tom and
George waiting at the gate. We paid for our admission, and when we
got in, found the grounds occupied by a Sunday School out for a treat.
There were hundreds of children, who were being amused by their
35   teachers and parsons in every imaginable way. We much enjoyed the
scene; at one time I was sitting down with two little mites of children,
sitting one on each of my knees, when one of the parsons came by, and
said I was a good shepherd looking after the sheep. I thanked him, and
he passed on. There were several girls there, who I think were
40   teachers, with whom we got into conversation, and asked them
whether they would start a game of "Kiss in the Ring", in which we

could join. They did so, but immediately the ring was made, it was joined by scores of yelling little wretches, so we declined. We intended to have gone up the Wynd Cliff, on the opposite side of the river, where there is a fine view to be obtained, only the weather looked queer, so we stayed where we were. We left the Castle, (the ruins of which are very extensive and picturesque) at 7.30. Whilst Fred and I walked home together, we saw a girl bobbing an apple to her little sister. I asked her whether she would bob it to me; she said she would, and after many knocks on the nose, I managed to get a mouthful, much to the amusement of them both. We had supper at 8, chops. Afterwards Fred and I wrote some letters, and then went out to post them. We had a good deal of trouble to find the pillar box, but were assisted in our search in the dark by some girls, who then asked for some money for beer, and as we declined to give it, there was a row. We went to bed at 10.30; Fred and I slept together, and the other three were in a double-bedded room.

Thursday, August 12th

We were called at 4, dressed, packed up, and came down to a capital hot breakfast of chops at 4.30: when we had finished, we took out traps, and went down to the workshop where we had taken the boat the night before, and found James had made a very good job of the broken stern, having bound it round with copper plates: we carried it down the steps and put it in the water, and the fishing boat with the two boatmen having come alongside, we put all out things in it and started away at 5.15 with our own empty boat in tow. George and Fred thought they would like to keep themselves warm, so they used our pair of oars, and assisted the boatmen. Of course it poured with rain, and the wind was bitterly cold, so we were glad to have our macintoshes on. I steered and Tom and Clarke sat with me in the stern, so we huddled up together with the rug over our knees, and kept ourselves as warm as possible. There was a good tide with us, so we soon got over the three miles of river, and into the open water which was very lumpy, the boats rising and falling in the troughs of the waves, showing us how absurd it would have been for us to have ventured across alone. On several occasions our boat which was towing behind was lifted up by the waves, and thrown bow foremost onto the stern of the fishing boat, and once it came down with such force, that it broke the top of the rudder. The distance between the mouths of the Wye and the Avon is 9 miles, and we arrived at our destination about 8 o'clock, when we suddenly discovered that we had left the stern rail of the boat at Chepstow. I volunteered to go back and fetch it, and the boatmen saying that I might return with them, I accepted their offer, and told the others to meet me in the afternoon at Bristol Railway Station. On arriving at the Avon mouth, the boatmen ran their boat ashore on the mud to keep it steady, and we then trans-shipped everything into our boat: Clarke and Tom got out the sculls, and after paying the men, they started up the river, leaving me behind.

The men found very considerable difficulty in getting the boat off the mud, as while the others had been removing the things, the tide had fallen and left us almost high and dry, however, by dint of great deal of moving with the oars, and one of the men getting out and pushing, we managed to get afloat again, and turned back towards Chepstow,   5
the men pulling and I steering them. We had the tide against us, and after rowing for about 6 miles, we got astern of a trawl that was making for the Wye, and took us in tow. My services not being required any longer at the tiller, and the sun having come out, I went to sleep. We kept astern of the trawl until we entered the river, when   10
the tide having turned and commenced to run up, we cast off and the men recontinued rowing. Near the mouth of the river I saw 18 boats all in a row, with one man in each, salmon fishing, with nets which spread underneath the boats. One of boatmen told me that a man sometimes caught 130 to 150lbs of salmon in a day, and this he could   15
sell at -/10 to a 1/- per lb. In the river the tide was almost dead low, and on either side were high mud banks, which looked extremely ugly. At one place about a mile from Chepstow, I saw about 15 to 20 little boys plunging about in the mud without their clothes: they had made a slide down the muddy bank about 20 feet long, and they took it   20
in turns to slide down on their backs into a hole at the bottom, where they landed with a splash. We reached Chepstow at 10.45; I left the boat and found old James, who was very much surprised to see me. I told him what I wanted, and after a short search we found the rail in the workshop. James told me he thought I could just catch a train if I   25
went to the station at once, so I hurried there as fast as I could, but

found that I had to wait 80 minutes: I amused myself by writing home
on some of the Railway Excursion Handbills, and begged an envelope
from a man in the Booking Office. At 12.20, a train came in, which
took me to Portskewett, where I arrived at 12.30; I had to change
there, and on enquiring found I had to wait until 1.50. I was very
hungry by this time, having had nothing since 4.30, but there was no
refreshment room, so I had to grin and bear it. At 1.50, I got into a
train which took me to the Pier Head, where I embarked on board a
steamer, and crossed the Severn, the passengers staring at me as if I
were a wild beast. On arrival at the other side, I got into another train,
and arrived at Bristol at 3.15: Tom and Fred met me at the station and
we walked to the "Talbot Hotel" where they had put up, and on our
arrival, Tom carried the rail down to the boat house. Of course the
others had had their dinner, so I had mine alone, and I made the
waiter open his eyes very considerably at the way in which I put it
away. The others related to me what had happened after we separated,
which can be told in a few words. Tom and Clarke started sculling and
they pulled up to Pill, opposite to which was our inn called the
"Lamplighters", much frequented by pilots and seafaring men: they
drew the boat up on to the hard, went into the inn, and had a capital
breakfast of coffee, bread and butter: they stopped there about an
hour, waiting for the tide to help them up to Bristol. They started
again, and sculled under Clifton Suspension Bridge, 300 feet above
them; the water about there runs nearly black, and smelt very
disagreeably. A great many people collected on the bridge, and at the
Railway Station to stare at them as they went by. They found the lock
gates of the basin closed, and were told that they would not be opened
until high tide, an hour or two later, and as the river was barred
beyond, they got some men to assist them to carry the boat over the
quay on a trolley, and lower it into the river again, about 200 yards
further up. They then sculled on for two miles, having to steer very
carefully on account of the number of ships and steamers which were
shifting and steaming about, and arrived at the Club Boat House
about 12, they left the boat there, walked to the Talbot Hotel, which
was close by, engaged rooms, and had dinner. After I had finished my
dinner and changed my clothes, we all started out for a long walk: we
had not gone very far before we missed Clarke, who had lagged
behind, we looked about for him, but could see nothing of him, so we
went on to the Cathedral, which we found in a state of great confusion,
as there was a new nave being built, and the building was blocked up
in many places: the roof was very handsome, as also were some of the

arches: we were shown some curiously carved chorister stalls, very much after the same style as those we saw in Holy Trinity Church, Stratford on Avon: just outside the Cathedral were the ruins of the Archbishop's Palace, which was completely destroyed during the Chartist Riots. We walked to Clifton, which was a long way, all up hill, and a very tiring journey: as we arrived near the Suspension Bridge, a heavy shower came on, so we took refuge in a refreshment

room which was close to hand, and waited there until it was over: we then went to see the bridge, and the view of the bridge and the river from the rocks above: we sat down on a bench for some little time admiring the view, and then turned homewards. We had only gone a short distance when it began to rain again, and we took shelter in the back entrances of some houses, but we got tired of waiting, so turned up our collars, and started off at a run: in a very few minutes, however, it come down in such torrents that we were obliged to stand up for shelter in a row under some small trees with our backs against a wall just in front of some houses; various of the inmates were at the windows looking at us in our queer and uncomfortable positions, but not one of them invited us to come in out of the wet, so when the water

gently trickled on us through the trees, we made up our minds for a
soaking and walked home; of course we got wet through, and to add to
our annoyance we found Clarke taking it easy in the smoking room, as
dry as a bone. We dried ourselves and Fred went to see an Aunt who
lived at Clifton; we had some tea, and in the evening went into the
Billiard Room, and played a few games among ourselves. We were
very tired and turned in at 10.30, Fred and I slept together, George
and Tom in another room and Clarke by himself. The Talbot Hotel
had only recently been built, everything was very nice and new, and
the attendance and grub were excellent.

Friday, August 13th

Got up at 8, had breakfast at 8.45, chops; paid our bill, and
George, Tom, Clarke and I went down to the boathouse, Fred having
gone immediately after breakfast to visit some more of his relations.
We got everything ready, and waited impatiently for Fred, who
presently appeared in a tremendous heat. We got away at 10. 10, and
rowing through the town, soon got into the Avon again through an
open lock. Tom and I then sculled for six miles. When we arrived at
Hanham Lock, where we had been instructed to apply for a canal pass
to Reading, on application, however, we were told that we should get
it at Twerton Lock, some distance further on. We went on for 2½
miles, and arrived at Keynsham Lock. Here we found that our winch
was much too small to fit the windlasses; a much larger one being
required on the Avon, and on the Kennet and Avon Canal, so we gave
the lock-keeper half a crown, and he supplied us with an extra one that
he had, which would fit all the locks, and which we found to be of
immense service to us. I landed at Keynsham, and bought half a gallon
of milk at a public house. I asked whether they could let me have any
bread, but as they could only let me have a stale loaf, I declined. They
told me there was a shop distant about three minutes walk, where it
was sold, so Fred started off to find it, and bought some new loaves.
When we had all reassembled, we went on through some more locks,
and looked out for a convenient place to bathe. It was some time before
we found a spot sufficiently private, but at last we came to a place
where there was some splendidly deep water, and although there was a
footpath running along the bank, it was well sheltered by many willow
trees. We ran the boat in between two of these trees, and Clarke began
his bathe first, by sticking his leg in the water as he was getting ashore.
We undressed upon the bank and were soon all in the water, and had a
splendid bathe. We dried ourselves by running about in a field in the
sun. When we had finished we sculled a little further, until we came to

a nice quiet orchard reaching down to the water's edge. We pulled in
here alongside the bank, and as we saw nobody about, Fred and I
landed, and lay down on a rug. We got out the grub, and had lunch,
Fred and I supplying the others with a very plentiful supply of dessert
5   from the fruit trees which were very handy. We arrived at Twerton
Lock at 4.15, and procured our pass to Reading which cost 30/-. Two
miles further on we came to Bath, and as we were rowing through the
lower part of the town, the inhabitants came out in hundreds to look at
us, but we were pretty well used by that time to being stared at. We
10 had been recommended to a man named Hooper, who, we were told,
would take charge of our boat, so we pulled up to his garden which
was situated just below the seven locks which lead up to the Kennet and
Avon Canal. It was a filthy dirty garden, and there was a wretched
little landing stage at the end of it, to which several boats in the last
15 stages of decomposition were attached. The man himself appeared,
when we shouted, and he looked as dirty as his house and garden. It
was five o'clock when we landed. We went up through the house,

crossed the river by a footbridge, and walked to the Christopher
Hotel, where we engaged rooms, and ordered supper. After we had
performed our necessary ablutions, Tom, Fred and I went to the Post
Office, and got the letters, and also the ordnance maps of the rest of
the route, which had been sent to us from London. Fred called in at   5

his uncles at Broad Street, and left Tom and me outside. We soon got
tired of waiting, so turned in to a public house opposite, and had some
liquor. The landlord insisted upon our having it in the parlour and
was very loquacious. He very much amused us by taking us for
cricketers, and indeed, most people that saw us in the streets thought   10
the same. On rejoining the others at the Hotel, Fred, George, Tom
and I sallied out to walk up the Beechen Cliff. Clarke did not
accompany us, but went to see his aunt, who lived in the town. On the
road up the hill we got into conversation with an old man, who took us
for sailors, and being rather tight, he was very amusing, and wished   15
us to go and drink the Queen's health with him. When we arrived at
the top of the cliff, we were well rewarded for our walk with a
beautiful view of the town and the surrounding country. The whole of

the buildings being built of stone, it had a very curious effect; everything looked gray. We went back into the town, and went over the Bathing Establishment, saw the pump room, hot springs, private baths, and tasted the waters. We returned at 8.30 to supper, and sat
5   down to a glorious spread of cold duck, lamb, roast and boiled beef, salad, tea and coffee, to which we did ample justice. We did not go out after supper as it rained, although during the whole of the day, the weather had been splendid, with a bright, hot sun. We studied the new maps, and went into the Billiard Room to smoke and have our
10   grog. Had several games of billiards, and went to bed at 11; Tom, Fred and I had a double-bedded room, and Clarke and George had separate rooms.

Saturday, August 14th

George, Tom and Fred got up at 8, went to the Bathing Establishment
and had a tepid swimming bath. They returned soon after 9, when
we had breakfast, cold lamb, cold boiled and roast beef and eggs.
We all thought we should like to have a photograph of the boat taken
as a momento of the trip, so after breakfast Fred and I walked to   5
the best photographers in the place, Flukes & Son in Milsom Street,
and arranged that they should meet us as 12 o'clock in Sydney Gardens
as the canal goes through these gardens, and we had therefore to pass
through them. On our way back, Fred called in to make his fond
adieu to his aunt, and when I got to the hotel, I found that Tom and   10

Clarke had gone to see the Abbey, which is situated close to the
"Christopher". Fred's aunt was not at home, so he very soon turned
up, and after we had paid the bill, and expressed our satisfaction to the
landlord, of the comforts of his hotel, he, George and I took our
luggage, and started away, leaving word for Tom and Clarke to
follow us on their return from the Abbey. We went down to Hooper's
cottage and found that, dirty as all his surroundings were, he had
found time to clean our boat out very thoroughly, and nicely. We
started off at 10.40. I stayed in the boat, and George and Fred landed
to open the locks of which there were seven very deep ones close
together connecting the river Avon with the Kennet and Avon Canal.
These took us an hour to get through. When we were at the third,
Tom and Clarke appeared. I took their luggage into the boat, and they
busied themselves in keeping back an immense crowd of children
which had collected, and impeded George and Clarke in their work.
When we had risen into the Canal, I took them all in the boat, and we
sculled into Sydney Gardens, which are very pretty. We found the
photographers waiting for us on the tow-path with two machines.
They were a long time getting ready, and as the boat would not keep
perfectly still, we tied the stern to either side of the bank. They took

two negatives, but as it turned out afterwards, they were wretched things, quite a failure. We gave them an address to send the proofs to, and left them. We sculled for two miles, then stopped at a little public house and bought some bread, butter and beer. I tried to get some milk, but the cows had not been milked, so I filled my can with fresh spring water. We then pulled along through some very fine scenery, and past a great number of stone quarries, until we arrived at Dundas Aqueduct, which is built over the River Avon, and the Great Western Railway. Fred and I got out, and from the Aqueduct we had a splendid view of the surrounding country. We looked about for a suitable lunching place, and having gone over the Aqueduct, and round a bend of the canal on the other side, we landed, spread the rug and cushions, on a grassy bank under the shadow of some trees, and got out the eatables etc. We had lunch, but were a good deal disturbed by the wasps, which surrounded us in great numbers, and kept on annoying us, especially Fred, who was on his legs every minute slashing at them with his hat like a maniac. Just opposite to us on the

other side of the water was a little cottage, and in the garden we saw some splendid apple trees. Fred and I, therefore, went across on a raft, which we found close by and bought some off the old woman that lived in the house. Whilst I was picking some, a bee stung me on the forehead. I immediately asked the old lady for a bluebag, which she fetched and was busy rubbing me with it when she uttered a yell, and said that she had also been stung on the face. Upon this I immediately decamped from the garden, and left Fred to pick the rest of the apples, which were very good. After we had finished lunch, Fred proposed a clamber up the hill, at the foot of which out boat lay. Clarke and George assented, and they went to the top from which they said there was a very fine view. Tom and I stayed behind to watch the boat, and we both went to sleep. The others returned at 4.30 with their pockets full of nuts, which they had picked from the trees; the majority of them were unripe, but some were very good. We got off again at 4.45, and saw a large batch of Charity children, who appeared to be out for a picnic. Soon after this we passed an orchard which was temptingly near so I got out and helped myself to some immense apples; however, the others did not appreciate them as they should have done, but said they were cooking apples. We passed over another aqueduct at Stoke and arrived at Bradford at 6. We intended staying there until Monday, so we got the boat through the lock, and went alongside a warehouse belonging to the Railway Company. It had a door opening onto the water, so we obtained permission from the office and handed the moveables in, tied the boat up, and the place was locked up. We marched through the town, which was being profusely decorated with triumphal arches, venetian masts, and flags, in preparation for a grand fete which was to be held there on the following Tuesday. We applied at several inns, but they could not accommodate so large a party; but eventually we found very good rooms at the Swan Hotel. We washed and changed, then strolled up to the Post Office, and through the streets. Had tea at 8, cold ham and eggs. Afterwards we smoked and read the papers. Turned in at 10.30, Fred and I slept together, George and Tom slept together, and Clarke had a room to himself. The weather all day had been splendid.

Sunday, August 15th

Got up at 9, and had breakfast at 9.30. We smartened ourselves up as much as possible, and at 11 o'clock went to the Old Church for morning service. There was a very large congregation, and a surpliced choir; but the singing was not up to much. We had a short stroll after church, and went back to dinner at 1, hot lamb, apple and black-currant tarts. After dinner Clarke had a nap, and George, Tom, Fred and I went for a walk on the bank of the river. We lay down in the shade under the trees and smoked; but the other three shortly left me and continued their walk, and very soon I fell asleep. About 4 I went back to the hotel, and found Clarke, George and Tom, but Fred, they said, had extended his walk, and had not returned. Clarke stood a bottle of champagne to speed the parting guest, as Tom had to return to town. We went down to the station, and saw him off by the 4.50 train, and wondered all the time where Fred was, as we fully expected he would come and say goodbye. Later on in the evening, Clarke, George and I went for a long walk in the country; lay down in some fields and enjoyed the cool of the evening. We returned at 8 to the hotel, and had tea. Fred had not turned up, and as he had disappeared for four hours, we began to get anxious about him, thinking that perhaps he had come to grief somewhere whilst out walking. We decided we would wait until 10, and then we would go to the Police Station, and institute a search. We smoked and read good books all evening, and at 10 we put on our hats to go to the Police Station, when in walked Fred, in a most unconcerned manner. When asked where he had been, he said to see his grandmother's grave, and gave similar evasive answers. We could get nothing satisfactory out of him, and considered it a case full of suspicion. We went to bed at 11.

Monday, August 16th

We got up at 7, had breakfast at 8, ham and eggs, walked down to the Railway Company's warehouse, and having got the boat ready, started off at 9. Just past Hilperton Marsh we ran into the bank, and had a splendid bathe, notwithstanding the numerous notice boards
5   which were placed at intervals along the banks. At Semington we went

ANY PERSON BATHING IN

THIS CANAL WILL BE LIABLE

TO A PENALTY OF 40 SHILLINGS

W. MERRIMAN

PRINCIPAL CLERK

through two locks and at Seend five more. Here we tried to get a cart or trolley at a farmhouse to take our boat by road to Devizes, as we wished to avoid going through the 29 locks which go up the hill to Devizes, but the woman at the farmhouse wanted 15/- for a horse and
10   trolley, and as we thought this a great deal too much, we declined her offer. We soon afterwards met a barge which was going our way, and the bargees suggested they should take our boat through the locks on their barge. To this suggestion we took very kindly, as it was fearfully hot, and they therefore took us in tow at once, and we went like this
15   for two miles, and although slow, it was a very easy and comfortable

mode of progression. On reaching the first of the locks we followed
the barge in, and when we had risen, we lifted our boat onto the
barge, by first bringing it close to the wall, then raising it, and whilst
it was suspended in the air, pushed the barge underneath, and lowered
it onto the timber with which the craft was loaded. We secured and
fastened it to the timber, and placed some sacks underneath the bow
and stern. It was then 1.30, and the men immediately began their
upward journey. Fred and I walked along the tow-path up the hill to
Devizes, which was two miles distant. When we reached the end of
the 29 locks, and consequently the top of the hill, on looking down,
there was a very fine view, and it looked very singular to see all the
locks one above another, occupying a distance of two miles, and
bringing the water up such a steep ascent. We walked into the town;
went to the Post Office, got the letters, bought some bread, butter and
fruit, and after having looked over the place, returned to the tow-
path, and waited for George and Clarke to come up. We had been
unable to get any milk at Devizes, so Fred and I got through a hedge,
and walked across a field to a small farmhouse, which we went into,
but found it occupied only by a lot of children, all of whom I noticed
had most enormous mouths, almost stretching from ear to ear. We
enquired of the eldest girl whether we could have some milk; she
replied that she would go and ask her mother, who was out. She
accordingly went, entrusting us with the charge of the children, whom
we promised to take care of, and with whom we immediately
fraternized and made great friends. The girl shortly came back with
the required permission, and we bought a gallon of milk. We rejoined
the others, and had lunch on a grassy bank under the shadow of some
trees, close by the tow-path, anxiously and earnestly watched the whole
time by a group of small children, to whom we afterwards gave the
remnants of the feast. The barge got through the last lock at 4.50; we
put our boat into the water again, gave the bargees half a crown for
beer, and sculled away, followed for some distance by a number of
children, who only gave up the chase through sheer exhaustion. After
sculling four miles we passed a boat containing three boys who were
rowing two ladies, and we also saw several other boats evidently
belonging to people whose gardens or grounds adjoined the canal.
Whilst stopping to have a drink, Fred dropped our best cup overboard
we endeavoured to fish it up, but it was no use, it could not be
recovered. George had previously dropped one of our pannikins
overboard at Hampton Lucy, so we were reduced to one pannikin for
the beer, and an old marmalade pot for the milk. The sun was so

fearfully hot, that we could hardly drink enough, and were constantly
stopping to liquor up. At All Cannings, very near the canal, we saw
another white horse cut in a green hill. It was an awkward looking
animal with a very long neck, and its legs all over the country. Close
5 by this we passed an outrigged boat with a lot of old ladies in it, and
also another boat with some girls rowing. We intended passing the
night at All Cannings, but it was such a little place, that we were told
we should certainly be unable to find accommodation there, and were
advised to go on to Honey Street, which we did, and arrived there at
10 8. It was a glorious evening, the sun was just setting; there was hardly
a breath of wind, and everything seemed calm and peaceful. George
and Clarke walked up the street to the Barge Inn, which was the only
one in the village; but they could not accommodate us, having "no
room for strangers". We were rather disconcerted at this rebuff, but
15 sculled on towards Wilcot Bridge, which was three miles further on.
It was getting dusk, and a full moon was rising, and it being such a
lovely evening, we enjoyed it immensely, although we were rather
anxious about our beds. When we arrived at Wilcot Bridge, George
and I walked to the village, and tried our luck at the Golden Swan.
20 Here, however, we were again doomed to disappointment, for they
only had one bed, and there was not another to be had in the place. We
therefore disconsolately returned to the canal, where Fred and Clarke
were waiting in the boat, as usual, the centre of observation of a large
crowd. After having been assured that we should obtain accommodation
25 at Pewsey, three miles further on, we started off again. By this time it
was quite dark, with the exception of the light from the moon, which
had risen, and as we passed through Wilcot Park, the effect was very
fine; the moon shining through the dark masses of underwood, and
silvering the water. We arrived at Pewsey at 9.15, and found some
30 men at the wharf, also a wharfinger, who took our pass to sign, saying
he would return it in the morning. We got the boat out of the water
and the wharfinger having placed a barn at our disposal, we carried it
inside, with all the belongings, and locked it up for the night. We
then shouldered our baggage, and walked to the town which was a
35 mile distant, along a pretty road. We had been recommended by the
wharfinger to the Phoenix Hotel, as being the best in the town, so we
went there and ordered supper to be got ready at once, as we were
ravenously hungry. The supper appeared in due course, ham and
eggs, but it was not served at all nicely. The tea was very bad, 'scented
40 Pekoe, Clarke pronounced it) and the other things were to match. It
was a beautifully warm evening, so after we had finished supper, Fred

and I went out for a walk outside the town. The moon made it almost as light as day, and it was most enjoyable strolling about and smoking. We sat on a gate, and amused ourselves with singing our favourite songs and choruses. We had a long chat with a countryman, and very soon afterwards the policeman came up and stared at us, and then began to converse. As we were returning, we missed our way, and went some distance down a wrong road. We had some difficulty in finding the right one, and did not get back to the hotel until 11.15. The landlady was standing at the open door waiting for us. She wanted to lock up and go to bed, and was rather cross that we were so late. The others had gone to bed some time before. Fred and I slept together, and George and Clarke in another room.

Tuesday, August 17th

Yesterday we passed through some perfectly different country to what we had been used to. The wooded banks gave place to downs, beautifully green and undulating to the banks of the canal. We were on very high ground, and could see the country for miles round from the tow-path, and even sometimes from the boat. Our being on this high ground was, of course, accounted for by the fact that we rose about 350 feet at Devizes, when we passed through the 29 consecutive locks. Pewsey was three years previously the scene of the Autumn manoeuvres. The landlord gave us lengthy descriptions of what had occurred at that time, and said that Prince Arthur had slept in the same bed that George and Clarke had occupied. The troops were reviewed just outside the town on the downs. I got up at 8, and went for a short stroll before breakfast, which we had at 9; the breakfast was very far superior to the supper which we had had the night before. After we had finished Fred went to the Post Office to send a telegram home saying that he should leave us, and be there in the evening. He had heard news at Bath about his business which would not admit of his staying away any longer, and although, of course, he was not best pleased, he made up his mind to go away from Great Bedwyn. This reduced our party to three, and was unfortunate, although, of course, we had got through the worst part of the hard work, and we should very soon be in the Thames, where it would be all plain sailing. We walked down to the yard by the canal, and the man who had given the boat house room the night before was on the lookout for us. He unlocked the barn, and after having cleaned out the boat, we launched it, packed the things in, and started away about 10. Having come so far beyond our mark the night before, we had an exceptionally easy day's work before us; only ten miles.

We went through two locks, then Clarke took the can, and went for some milk to a farmhouse. They had none to spare there, so he went to

another, and the mistress gave him a quart, but would not accept
payment for it. This was the second instance of generosity in this way
that we had had shown us. At one of the lock-houses I added a quantity
of fresh water to the milk to eke it out, as it was very hot, and we all
required an immense quantity to drink. In the morning George had   5
filled a can with a gallon, which he bought for fourpence, and was
greatly elated with the bargain he supposed he had made; but when we
tasted it, we found it quite sour, and had to throw it away.

   We had for some time seen Savernake Forest in the distance, and
we then rapidly approached it; just on its outskirts we came to the   10
Bruce Tunnel. This was a very much better one than any we had gone

through. It was lofty, built throughout entirely of brick, and had a
chain attached along one side, although we did not use it, as it was
wide enough to admit of George and myself to scull short. This tunnel
was not half a mile long, and was perfectly straight, so that we could   15

see completely through it, and we therefore did not light the lamp.
We amused ourselves as usual by singing as we went through with all
our might and main. When we got through, we tied the boat to the
bank, and Fred and I climbed up on the top of the tunnel, we took the
5　beer can with us, as we had been told that there was an hotel on the
top. We walked back some distance, and soon came to the Savernake
Forest Hotel, where we were greeted by about a dozen dogs with a
very noisy welcome; in fact, there appeared to be more dogs than
visitors in the house, although the barmaid told us that it was nearly
10　always full in the summer. It was a good sized house, standing quite
by itself, and about a mile from the forest.

　　Savernake Station is closeby the Hotel, also on the top of the tunnel.
We bought some bread, butter and beer, and went back with them to
the boat, and then lay down on the grass preparatory to having lunch.
15　Just as we were preparing for a nap, a passenger train arrived; but
stopped before going into the station immediately opposite us, and
within 50 feet of the boat. The passengers, with one accord, crowded
to the carriage windows to have a look, and had sufficient time for
severe criticism, as the train waited there for about five minutes. The
20　engine driver, by that time, I suppose, having satisfied his curiosity,
took them on into the station. We had lunch, and afterwards lay down
and smoked. Fred and I then went hunting for nuts, and George and
Clarke pushed the boat into the tunnel in the shade, and went to sleep.
Above the arch of the tunnel fixed in the brickwork was a large flat
25　stone, with the following inscription engraved on it: —

THE KENNET AND AVON CANAL COMPANY INSCRIBE THIS

TUNNEL WITH THE NAME OF

BRUCE

IN TESTIMONY OF THEIR GRATITUDE FOR THE UNIFORM AND

EFFECTUAL SUPPORT OF THE RIGHT HONOURABLE THOMAS BRUCE

EARL OF AYLESBURY AND CHARLES LORD BRUCE HIS SON

THROUGH THE WHOLE PROGRESS OF THIS GREAT NATIONAL WORK

BY WHICH A DIRECT COMMUNICATION WAS OPENED BETWEEN THE

CITIES OF LONDON AND BRISTOL

ANNO DOMINI 1810

We started away again at 2.30; George and I sculled on for about a
mile, and then came to 10 locks all close together. George and Clarke
got out and opened them, whilst Fred and I remained in the boat.

These locks were very difficult to manage. The sluices were very rusty
and they required two to raise them, having been evidently unused for
a long time. Fred and I did not trouble ourselves to scull between the
locks; there was a strong wind in our favour, so that one of us had only
to stand up and hold his coat out to the breeze, and the boat was carried   5
along quite rapidly. Fred's train was advertised for 4.40 from
Bedwyn, and we started from the tunnel early on purpose to have
plenty of time, but the locks had hindered us so much that we feared
he would lose the train. When, therefore, we neared the village, as the
rail was close to the canal, Fred and I landed, and got on the line. He   10
ran on to the station to get his ticket, and I followed behind with his
portmanteau. We got to the station at 4.45, five minutes late, but the
train did not come in for more than 20 minutes. I saw Fred off, and
returned to the canal, George and Clarke having arrived at the bridge.
George went into the village, and engaged rooms at the "Cross Keys".   15
We took the luggage out of the boat at a wharf close by the bridge, and
locked the boat up for the night in a barn. We found the Inn a very
comfortable little place, with a capital sitting room to ourselves. We
washed and changed, and I then went to the Post Office. Just as I
returned it commenced to rain. It had looked threatening all day; there   20
had not been much sun, but it had been very hot. We had to content
ourselves indoors in the evening; but we got some books, and
managed to pass away the time very comfortably. Had supper at 8,
chops and eggs, and went to bed at 10. George and I slept together,
and Clarke had a room to himself.   25

Wednesday, August 18th

We got up at 8.30, packed up, and came down to breakfast at 9. They had no more chops in the town, so we again had to content ourselves with bacon and eggs. Directly after breakfast I went down to the wharf, found a man there belonging to the place, and with his assistance got the boat into the water. I then put the things in order, and waited for the others. George and Clarke very soon appeared, having paid the bill which was only 14/9. The waitress was rather unsophisticated; George gave her a shilling; but she brought it back again and said that the attendance had been charged in the bill, and it was not until it was explained to her that it was for herself, that she appeared to comprehend.

We got away at 10: there were 10 locks to go through before we came to Hungerford, a distance of only five miles, so the lock-keeper, who had heard of our arrival the night before, and was waiting for us in the morning, went on ahead and helped us to open six of them. These locks were just as stiff and unmanageable as the others that were on the other side of Great Bedwyn. They were also very large and took a long time to fill. There was a fair wind, so we rigged up a sail on the tow-mast with a boathook and the rug, and went on between the locks without sculling; but afterwards the banks got high, so that the wind was not of much service to us, and as there were a great many very low swing bridges where we had to unship the mast each time, we soon gave it up. When we arrived at Hungerford Bridge, George and I got out, went into the town, and bought some bread and cakes at a confectioner's. I was unable to get any milk, so filled my can with water at the Public House, where George got his beer. When we returned to the boat we found it underneath the bridge, where Clarke in an excess of modesty had pushed it, to be out of sight to the crowd of people who had collected to look at him.

We sculled about a mile from the town, and found a nice secluded spot, where we thought to have a jolly bathe. The weeds, however, were very thick, so much so that we could not get a dive from any part of the bank, and we did not enjoy it so much as we might otherwise have done. I thought of bathing in the River Kennet, which, at that part ran parallel to the canal, but on examination, I found there was only about two feet depth of water, although it was quite free from weeds. After dressing we went a little further on, and it then commenced to rain. Clarke got out to open a lock. and whilst going through, I hurried over my lunch, and by the time he was in the boat again, I had finished so I fitted up the towmast, and after putting on my macintosh and sou'wester, got out and towed whilst the others had their lunch. The rain did not continue, only came down in one or two heavy showers, and the sun shortly came out again. At Kintbury, just as I was going over the bridge to open a lock, a very swell carriage was driven over with a parson and some ladies in it, who seemed much amused at my appearance, and no doubt I did present a peculiar figure, macintosh and sou'wester dripping wet, bare legs, and a heavy winch over my shoulder.

A short distance past Kintbury we met a large steam launch coming along the canal; there were several men on deck and some small children. We heards afterwards when we arrived at Newbury in the evening, that it was bound for Bristol, and had a brother of Capt. Boyton's on board. It appeared to get along very slowly, the weeds must have hampered the screw greatly. When we got to Hampstead Marshal I ceased towing, and got into the boat, when George and Clarke sculled. This was the first piece of towing we had done since we left the Hereford Gloucester Canal. The sun soon came out and dried our clothes, and allowed us to more thoroughly enjoy the beautiful scenery. We passed Frog Hall, and went right through the park, which is very well kept and is beautifully timbered. The last two locks before we reached Newbury took us an immense time to get through, although fortunately, we had plenty of time. For some 20 or 30 yards before we came to these locks, we found the water perfectly choked with weeds, that had been cut and were floating; it was impossible to open the gates until some had been cleared away, and then again, when the boat was inside, we could not close the gates, so we all three had to stand on the gates and with sculls and boathooks, push the weeds into the lock, and so manage to shut them. At the last lock, after having got through, one of the sluices got choked, and we could not let it down, so we had to leave the water running.

We reached Newbury at 6.45. Seeing a boathouse just before we

got to the town with some very antedeluvian boats moored there, we
enquired, and found we might leave ours there for the night. Just
above the town, the Kennet took the place of the canal, and flowed with
a pretty fair stream all the way to the Thames. Of course, the river was
5 locked, but the stream was kept up, and the surplus water discharged
by means of small weirs. The boatman recommended us to go to the
White Hart Hotel in the Market Place, so we took our traps and went
there. I changed my things, and went to the Post Office next door for
letters; ordered supper, and we all went for a stroll through the town.
10 It is a large place and an important business town. Clarke and I went
to a barber's, but could not persuade George to join us, whose chin
looked like a blacking brush. We went back to supper at 8.30, and
had some very good steak. We afterwards adjourned to the billiard
room. Clarke smoked and looked on, while George and I played a
15 couple of games. We turned in at 10.30; George and I slept together,
and Clarke was by himself.

Thursday, August 19th

We got up at 7.30. It was a fine morning; had breakfast at 8.15, cold chicken and ham. Clarke got the waitress to sew up his travelling bag which had burst open through much knocking about. We went out and bought a large plum cake for lunch; filled our cans with beer and milk, and started away at 9.15. There was a very low swing-bridge between the boathouse and Newbury Lock, which it would have been impossible to get under, so two of the boatmen went on and opened it for us. We went into the lock and got through. There was a lock-house there, but no lock-keeper, only an old woman, who asked us for our pass, and went to the wharf to get it signed. We waited for her for some time just opposite the stone bridge which goes over the canal, and which is in the principal street in the town. This bridge was soon crowded with people who stopped to stare at us, and see us start, and the windows of the houses near the water were also filled with wondering spectators. At last the old woman appeared with the signed pass, so we sculled under the bridge and away out of the town past numerous wharves. The first lock we came to was an enormous one, nearly large enough to hold a ship. It took a long time to fill; but there was a keeper there to assist us. We shortly afterwards went through two more about the same size, which hindered us a good deal. On approaching another swing-bridge and a lock a little further on, to save time, I took the winch and got out, running on ahead. I tried my best to swing the bridge round, but found it immovable. These bridges appeared to get lower the further we advanced, so we took the lounge rail off, and George and Clarke having laid themselves flat down in the bottom of the boat, they pushed through with their hands, and just managed to squeeze under. When I came to examine the locks, I found that the winch would not be the slightest use, as it was a bar lock, that is, a lock with four wooden sluices in each gate. The handles had holes punched in them, and it was necessary to have a heavy crowbar to fit in the holes and prise the sluices up out of the water. I looked everywhere for the bar, but could not find it. I then tried all manner of ways to get the sluices up, and thought the handle of the winch would manage it; but I could not move them an inch. At last I gave it up in despair, and we had no alternative but to carry the boat round. We therefore, with as little delay as possible, took everything out of the boat, placed the rollers in position, rolled it round and launched it at the other side. This was very stiff work for three, and took us a long time, for the lock was a very large one, and we had no extra hands to throw up and place the rollers. However, we managed it at last, and devoutly hoping that we should not meet any more obstacles, proceeded. The swing-bridges were now more frequent than ever, and going under one, we stuck in the middle, and it was with the greatest difficulty we got out again. We highly amused some girls who were looking at us from the bank, by our movements when we came to a bridge. At a call from the coxswain, the sculls were immediately shipped, and we all three disappeared into the very bottom of the boat. We asked them to come in and try the sensation, but I suppose they preferred watching without incurring any risk. Just above Coldthrop Mill we saw a man coming along the tow-path, who stopped when he saw us, and then ran on ahead; whilst doing so he dropped his dinner which he had tied up in a handkerchief; we told him of it and he came back and picked it up. He then said that he was a locksetter, and would run on the open the next lock for us. He opened the one at Coldthrop Mill, (this was a large paper mill) and also the next at Midgham, which was half a mile further on. He then expressed his intention of running on and preparing the next, which was two miles ahead. As this was likely to prove warm work for him, we offered him a seat in the boat, which he gladly accepted. We therefore stowed him away in the bow, and Clarke and I sculled on to Aldermaston; but we found he weighed very solid. He open this lock for us, and said that although the next one was not under his care, he would go on with us, as it was a bar lock, and he knew where a crowbar was kept. We accordingly went on there, and he fished it out of a tree, which accounted for my not being able to get hold of one at the previous bar lock. I asked him whether he couldn't let us keep the bar, and after some demure he gave it up on condition I gave it back to the next setter. This I promised to do, and he went away very well satisfied with the shilling we gave him for his trouble. There being another lock half a mile further on, I took the winch and walked along the towpath to get it ready whilst the others sculled after me. As I was passing a cottage on the bank of the canal, (the occupants of which as usual had turned out in force to watch the approach of the boat), an old woman suddenly dived back into the house, and (doubtless comprehending the hungry look with which I eyed an apple tree in the garden) reappeared with a lot of apples, which she begged me to accept. Of course I did not require twice asking, and I quickly demolished them as they were very good. She also gave some to George and Clarke when they passed in the boat. It was not often we came across such well-dispositioned old females. Just opposite the village of Southampstead Bannister we lay up under the bank and devoured the cake which we were quite prepared for, as it was then 3.45. We hurried over our lunch, and after passing through two more locks, arrived at another bar-lock. I had taken a lesson from the setter how to manage them, but it took me a considerable time to lift the sluices, and even then the lock was so large, and the gates so leaky that it was a long while before it filled. We all three had to tackle the gate, which was awfully stiff. When we were four miles from Reading we came across another setter, who gave us the welcome news that there were no more bar-locks on the canal. I therefore gave him back the crowbar, which he was rather surprised to see in our possession. We were quite overjoyed to find that we should be troubled with no more bar-locks, as we understood there were several near Reading, but the setter told us that as these wore out, they were always replaced by winch locks, as the others were such a nuisance, and they always had to hide the bars, as the children either stole them or pitched them into the water.

Shortly after 7 o'clock, we arrived at the last lock on the canal belonging to the Canal Company, a brand new one, only very recently finished. I got out with the winch, and called out to a man who was standing on the gate to move, as I was going to shut it. He replied that I should not shut it, as he had just opened it for his barge which was coming down the canal. We had no time to waste, so I did not argue with him, but shut the gate with him on it, and let down the sluices, while George opened them at the other gate. The individual was greatly incensed at first, and seemed as if he would show fight, but thought better of it, and said he would fetch the lock-keeper to us, which he did; but by the time he had returned we were just out on the other side, so that they could not do much. We gave up our pass, which we did not require any more, and went on. We sculled right through Reading, a most dirty part of the town, with crowds of women and children looking at us, and soon arrived at the Thames

Conservancy Lock, which is quite near the mouth of the river. We had to pay to go through this. We passed under the Great Western Railway Bridge, and sculled into the Thames at 7.36; two miles above Sonning which we had on our programme as our halting place for the
5 night. It was quite a change getting into civilized places again, where we were not stared at, and where we saw other pleasure boats. Just

after we passed through Sonning Lock, and were in sight of the bridge, the rain suddenly came down in torrents. We covered up the luggage with the tarpaulin, but thought it useless to put on our
10 macintoshes, as we were already wet through. We went on, therefore, under the bridge, turned sharp round to the left under the footbridge, and up the back-water to the "French Horn", where we intended to pass the night. We went in and saw Hull, the proprietor, who told us he could put us up, so we took the cushions out of the boat and gave
15 them to the stable boy to dry. We took our luggage into our rooms, changed our clothes, and sent them to the kitchen to be dried. Had supper at 8.46, ham and eggs. Afterwards I renewed my acquaintance with "Spot" and his wife, who both snored nearly as much as Clarke. We smoked until 10.15, then went to bed pretty well tired out. This
20 had been the hardest day's work we had had: the locks we went through were all very large, more than twice the size of those on other

canals, the paddles were very stiff, nearly always taking two to move them, and as usual we had to fill all the locks before we went in, as the rule of the canal is always to leave them empty. The reason of this rule nobody appeared to know. Combined with these difficulties was the fact that there were only three of us to do the work. There was positively no trade at all on this canal between Devizes and Reading. We did not meet a single barge the whole of the distance. Between Bath and Devizes, the only reason they use barges is to fetch the stone from the quarries, which are generally quite close to the water. We were told that the Great Western Railway Company leased the canal, so as to keep the traffic on their line.

Friday, August 20th

I got up at 7, went across the bridge into the village to the Post Office, and got the letters. It was a most lovely morning after the rain. When I got back to the French Horn, I turned my attention to the boat, which, on examination, I found to be half full of water, as the
5   rain had come down in torrents all the night. I got the water out of it, and gave it a thorough washing and cleaning; then fetched the cushions which had been dried during the night, and put everything in the boat ready for starting. I took the fenders up to George in our bedroom, and he pipeclayed them. After they were done, however,
10 they did not look particularly white, as they had had some tremendous

soakings with the rain. We had breakfast at 9, ham and eggs, and got
away at 10. We sculled down to Marsh Lock, and whilst going in, our
flag again came to grief; snapped off sharp. The staff had by this time
got very short; but we stuck it in again in the bow and it looked very
little the worse. When we arrived at Henley we landed a little past the   5

bridge, and George and I got out and went in to the "Little White
Hart" to get some drink. He had his can filled with beer, and as there
was no milk to be had there, the landlord sent his son to a friend of his
with instructions if he had no milk to squeeze half a gallon out of a
cow. We then went up into the town, leaving Clarke in the boat, and   10
bought a cake and some fruit. By the time we came back, the boy had
returned with the milk, so we started off again soon after 12. It was
such a lovely morning, and the sun was so hot that we could not
manage without a bathe, so we made up our minds to go down to a
creek just below Medmenham Abbey, where we knew there was a   15
good place. We accordingly went there; but much to our surprise
found the place occupied by three girls in a boat. We landed, but they
did not go away, so I got my towel out, and flourished it about, then
examining the diving board, and finally took off my coat. It then
appeared to dawn on them what we wanted to do, for they suddenly   20

got out their sculls, and, much to our relief, decamped, leaving us
alone. We did not wait long before we were in the water. It was a
splendid place; 16 feet of water, and a board for diving. We stayed in
about half an hour, and after we had dressed, got out the grub, and
5 had lunch under the trees. Very soon after we had commenced, three
other fellows came across the fields from the direction of the Abbey, and
they also bathed. After lunch we lay down on the grass, and smoked
and slept alternately until 4 o'clock, then thought it time to move on.
Just as we were putting the things in the boat, the three girls I had
10 frightened away reappeared. We had occupied the place for two hours
and a half, so considered it was their turn. We assisted them out of
their boat and went away, leaving them in quiet possession. We
noticed they had rods with them, and were going to fish, we had
therfore unintentionally wasted all their ground bait, for after bathing,
15 we had seen a lot on the bank, and not knowing who it belonged to,
Clarke and I had shied it at each other. We went through Temple
Lock, the weir of which is considered one of the prettiest on the river,

and a little below passed a punt which contained four chairs, on which
were seated two amorous couples, who had their arms round each
20 other's waists, and were coo-ing away in a most affectionate manner.

This was in broad daylight on the open river. The old boatman, who was punting them along, kept his back most religiously turned on them, but was evidently much amused and enjoyed it immensely, as he kept winking and laughing at us. We were in fits of laughter, it looked so ridiculous. The whole lot of them appeared to be rather ancient,   5
and the women were awfully ugly. We arrived at Cookham at 6,

landed in the garden of the "Ferry Hotel", and I went in to enquire about accommodation. This hotel is very nice; everything is always very good. The rooms are comfortable, and it is beautifully situated, with a garden leading down to the river. It is therefore nearly always   10
full in summer. We were fortunate enough, however, to secure a double-bedded room, which George and I occupied, and Clarke slept out in the village, there being no other unoccupied bed in the hotel. We took out the luggage, and I sculled the boat round to the Boat Yard, and left it there for the night. I then changed my things, and ordered   15
supper at 8. Clarke soon came back from his cottage, looking very hot and red in the face, probably having had a tremendous struggle with his jersey, although he wouldn't own to it. He had the misfortune to have an exceedingly tight jersey, and it was with the utmost difficulty

that he could get it off by himself, one of us, therefore, almost always had to undertake the office of "peeling" him in the evening, and it was no rare occurrence to see him sometimes appear in another bedroom in a state of "semi-peel", and ask to be finished. We went in to supper at 8, when a steak pie was set before us, which we soon put away and asked for another. The servant stared, but brought another one, which soon followed the first. After supper we went out in the garden, and sat down by the water underneath the trees, and spent a most enjoyable evening. It was deliciously cool, and the moon added to the beauty of the scene. We stopped out there until past 11, chatting and smoking, then went to bed.

Saturday, August 21st

I got up at 7, and went down into the garden. It was again a most
lovely morning; the sun was already streaming down with tremendous
heat. George and Clarke shortly arrived also. I found a punt, and
punted Clarke across the river to where our boat had been moored the
previous night, and fetched it across. We fetched our towels, and got   5
into the boat, not troubling to put the cushions in, and George and I
sculled along the private water to Odney Pool. We stopped just above
the weir, leaving the boat, whilst we went round to the dressing shed.
We had a most enjoyable bathe, this being, in my opinion, the finest
bathing place on the river. A couple of spring-boards had lately been   10

placed there by the Cookham Swimming Club. There were a great
many other fellows there bathing, and among them I came across an
old school-fellow of mine, who accosted me in the water just as I had
risen from a dive. He was staying at Cookham for a few weeks. When
5   we were sculling back, George discovered that he had left his towel
behind; but as it belonged to the Hotel we thought it not worth while
going back for it. We got back to the Hotel at 8.0, and at 9 partook of
a capital breakfast, fried soles, grilled chicken, bacon and eggs, and,
of course, tea and coffee. We did justice to this, and I then went to see
10 about getting the boat ready, whilst the others paid the bill, which they
did with a great amount of satisfaction, as everything we had had was
very nice, and the Hotel altogether capitally managed.

We started away at 10, and I sculled down to the Lock, where there
was a girl talking to the keeper, and asking him whether there was not
15 some way of getting to Cookham without being obliged to walk, as she
and her sisters had already walked for more than an hour, and were
ready to drop with fatigue. The keeper replied that he didn't keep a
carriage, and that she would have to walk if she wanted to get there at
all. It struck me that it would be polite to offer to take her back to
20 Cookham, but when I saw the formidable array of young sisters, my

heart grew hard, and I didn't suggest it to the others, so I suppose they walked. The lock-keeper afterwards remarked that if her legs were as "lissome" as her tongue, she would find very little difficulty in doing the distance. I proposed that I should scull alone down to Maidenhead, so that Clarke should be the better able to enjoy the scenery. He 5 therefore lay down in the bow, whilst George steered me. It was very delightful going down the river past Cleveden, the scenery there is so

lovely, and the weather was so fine, that we thoroughly enjoyed it. I sculled very gently, and we did not keep the ordinary course of the stream, but went close to the bank opposite the tow-path, and in and 10 out among the little islands which were dotted about. I spun out the distance between Cookham and Maidenhead as long as possible, as we were not anxious to get out of the shade of the trees; the sun at that time coming down with tremendous force. We went through Boulter's Lock, and just after passing under Maidenhead Bridge, I pulled 15 ashore, and George and Clarke landed to get our day's lunch. I stayed in the boat until their return. They had only been able to obtain some beer, nothing whatever to eat. They had found a public house, but no shops. The town of Maidenhead is about a mile from the river, and there are only private houses down near the water. We then pulled 20

easily, (for it was blazing hot) down to Windsor, past the Eton
Bathing place, which looked very tempting, but there were too many
boats about for us to indulge. We went under the bridge, and landed
at some stairs, where Clarke and I got up, and went into the town,
5   walking up the hill leading to the Castle. We looked everywhere, but
could not see a dairyman's shop, so at last in desperation, we went into
a very small confectioner's, and bought some fruit and a cake, for
which we were charged about double as much as we ought to have
paid. I then enquired where I could get some milk, and found that I
10   need not go any further, as I could be supplied there with half a
gallon. On examination, afterwards, I discovered however, that I had
been given about a quart instead. It was very evident that we were
nearing London! It was the proprietor of the shop who served, an
awful swell in his way, and because I told him to "hurry up", I
15   suppose he took offence, and thought he would pay me out. We went
back to the boat, and found George gently grilling in the sun; woke
him up, and got away at 1. I suggested that we should go to my
favourite spot at Datchet Bridge for lunch. This is a very pretty place
just below the bridge; immediately after going through you turn sharp
20   off to the left up a litle creek where a boat can be safely moored out of
the stream, on the peninsular there is a fine old tree, under which is a

capital spot for lunching. The Home Park is exactly opposite on the other side of the river, and Windsor Castle can be seen in the distance through the arches of the bridge. We devoured our lunch, and afterwards lay down to enjoy a comfortable nap in the shade; but we were soon disturbed by the appearance of two small urchins with fishing rods. I tried to frighten them away with dreadful threats of having them locked up for trespassing, but it had little or no effect. I then asked one of them to lend me his rod, and after some little time, much to his astonishment, and very much more to mine, I succeeded in catching eight small fish. George and Clarke struck with envy at my success had a try with the other boy's rod, but they caught nothing except weeds. We packed up and started down the river again at 3.30; pulled gently past Staines down to Penton Hook Lock, and just after

we got through, George and I, who were sculling, had a smart spin with a pair down to Chertsey Lock, about 2½ miles. We left Penton Hook some 30 yards ahead, which we maintained to the finish. On arriving at Chertsey, we went into the creek which leads to the Boat House and Hotel. This was about 6 o'clock. On previous occasions, we had always put up at the "Cricketers Inn", the "Chertsey Bridge

Hotel" being generally full, but this time we obtained accommodation
at the latter place, and much did we regret it. There was only one
unoccupied bedroom, this, however, had three small beds in it. It was
the outside room of two. The inside room contained also three beds,
and the occupants had to go through our apartment before they could
get to their's, which would have been awkward, if we had happened to
have been ladies. After having changed my clothes, I went across to
the "Cricketers", and asked the landlord for a letter which I expected
from Tom. It told me that he and a friend, Ted White, were coming
to meet us the next day, and would arrive at 11 o'clock at Shepperton,
where I was to meet them, as there were no convenient trains to
Chertsey on Sunday. After some little time, George and Clarke joined
me in the garden. We ordered supper at 8, and then strolled into the
town which is about a mile from the river. We bought a large cake for
next day's lunch, and made arrangements about getting some milk in
the morning. Clarke and I went to a barber's and had a shave, but
George positively refused to have himself made to look decent about
the chin. At 8 we returned to the Hotel expecting to find supper ready;
but there were no traces of it. We waited and waited until past 9, abuse
seeming to have not the smallest effect on the waiters; however, about
9.30, we managed to get a first instalment. Sitting at the next table to
us was a party of three; two gentlemen and a girl. These had ordered a
very swell dinner, and they were positively worse off then we were.
We only expected a supper, and got it after a fashion. They expected a
good dinner, and after all, only got the same as we had. It was very
amusing to hear the elder of the two men continually pitching in to the
waiters. The soup was cold, he said; the fish was salt; the entrées were
burnt; and the wine was vile. He begged one of the waiters to oblige
him by tasting a potato, but the waiter, probably knowing more about
it than he cared to say, firmly but respectfully declined. Eventually
they brought a cold joint of meat, which we had long been waiting for,
so we fraternized with our ill-used friends at the next table, and ate
from the same joint. After supper we went out in the garden which
looks on to the river, smoked and listened to some niggers, who were
performing for the benefit of the visitors. We stayed out of doors until
10.45, then went to bed. We had to leave our door unlocked to allow
the other three fellows to get to their room, but they were not long
after us.

Sunday, August 22nd

I had an awfully bad night, kept waking up at all hours, thanks to
Clarke who snored and ground his teeth like a maniac all the night.
This was the first time I had slept in the same room with Clarke, and I
was very glad it was the last. We got up at 7, took towels, went across
the bridge to the weir and bathed. It was very jolly, the river just there   5
being very wide, and a tremendous rush of water from the weir. We
went back to the Hotel and ordered breakfast, and after bullying the
waiters and waiting nearly an hour, we got some. It was quite on a par
with the supper we had the night before; everything very bad and
served in a most uncomfortable style. The coffee was about the   10

substance of mud, the bread was stale and the ham was very salt. The
three egg-cups which we used appeared to be the only ones the
establishment possessed, as some other fellows that were having their
breakfast at another table in the coffee room, had their eggs brought in
5   in wine glasses. We asked for a slop basin. The waiter looked as if he
thought it quite an unnecessary luxury, and brought us a finger-glass,
that, I suppose, being the nearest substitute he could find. After
breakfast, whilst the other two packed up and got the boat ready, I
walked to the town with my can, and bought half a gallon of milk.

10   Directly after I returned we started away at 10.30, and sculled to
Shepperton Lock. I got out there, walked along the tow-path towards
the village, was ferried across, and then walked to the station. Just as I
was going in, I met a man I knew who was staying there for the
summer. The train from town arrived soon after 11 with Tom and
15   Ted. We walked to the river and found George and Clarke in the boat
waiting in the shade under some trees. We all embarked and George
and Tom sculled down the river to an island just above Sunbury Lock,
which we reached about 12. We got out, tied the boat up, and

prepared for lunch, which was on a rather more extensive scale than usual, as, besides our cake, beer and milk, Tom had brought with him in a bag, a lot of sandwiches, some apples, and a couple of bottles of champagne. Before we commenced lunch, a strolling photographer appeared, and begged us to allow him to take a group. George, Clarke   5
and Ted did not think it proper to be taken on Sunday, but Tom and I, overcoming our religious scruples, consented. The photographer, (who was a most curious looking individual, and who had an immense amount of small talk at his command), vanished among the trees, and shortly returned with a large box containing his apparatus, and his   10
friend and partner, whom he introduced as "Mr. 'Ill". Tom and I arranged ourselves in a group, and we were taken in two positions. One was just about as bad as the other, but I had to buy one. I put this in my bag, and afterwards found that in consequence of my having put it there while it was still rather wet, Tom's head had adhered to the   15
cover of my notebook, and the picture was consequently rather spoilt by one of the figures being decapitated. We lounged about on the island during the afternoon, smoking, talking, drinking and sleeping. It was a tremendously hot day, and we were glad to be in the shade during the hottest part of the afternoon. We stayed there until 4; then   20

started off again, Tom and I sculling until we arrived at Moulsey
Lock, when George and Clark relieved us, and they pulled to
Teddington, which we reached about 6. Fred, the boatman, received
us, and was rather astonished at our bronzed appearance. We changed
our clothes, not liking to be seen on Sunday evening going home in
our flannels. We left the cans, rollers, winches and flag (which looked
rather grubby) in our locker. We went to the station, and caught the
6.57 train to town. We left Clarke at Richmond, changed on to the
Hammersmith Line, and arrived home at 8.30.

SIR,—It has been suggested to me by several friends that the inclosed
information might be acceptable to many of your readers. I therefore
send you a tabular form, showing the particulars of a rowing tour which
was made and enjoyed by four friends and myself in the summer of last
year. Everyone who frequents the river Thames will have noticed the
large number of crews who are seen annually doing the trip by boat from
Oxford to London, but after this has been accomplished once or twice, one
naturally seeks for some further field of operations: to those, therefore,
I would suggest this tour, which to many would be a complete novelty,
and which leads through some most beautiful country, notably the course
of the Warwickshire Avon, and the valley of the Wye. I think the figures
below may be relied upon, the distances having been carefully taken from
Ordnance maps.   H. H. W.
Sept. 30, 1876.

Date.	Days' Routes.	Rivers and Canals.	Miles	Locks	Tunnels.
July 31	Oxford to Heyford	Oxford and Warwick Canal	17	10	...
Aug. 1	Heyford to Fenny Compton	Ditto and River Cherwell	28	19	...
2	Fenny Compton to Warwick	Ditto, Warwick and Nepton Canal, and River Avon	32	32	...
3	Warwick to Hampton Lucy	River Avon	10	...	...
4	Hampton Lucy to Fish and Anchor	Ditto	21	7	...
5	Fish and Anchor to Tewkesbury	Ditto	32	10	...
6	Tewkesbury to Newent	River Severn, and Hereford and Gloucester Canal	26	8	...
7	Newent to Hereford	Hereford and Gloucester Canal	31	14	3*
8	Stayed at Hereford				
9	Hereford to Ross	River Wye	30	...	...
10	Ross to Whitchurch	Ditto	14	...	...
11	Whitchurch to Chepstow	Ditto	27	...	...
12	Chepstow to Bristol	River Wye, across mouth of Severn, and River Avon	21	...	...
13	Bristol to Bath	River Avon	20	7	...
14	Bath to Bradford	Kennet and Avon Canal	13	8	...
15	Stayed at Bradford				
16	Bradford to Pewsey	Ditto	28	37	...
17	Pewsey to Great Bedwin	Ditto	10	16	1
18	Great Bedwin to Newbury	Ditto	18	22	...
19	Newbury to Sonning	Ditto, River Kennet, and River Thames	21	22	...
20	Sonning to Cookham	River Thames	19	6	...
21	Cookham to Chertsey	Ditto	23	9	...
22	Chertsey to Teddington	Ditto	13	4	...
		Total	454	331	4

* One of these tunnels is about 1½ miles in length.

Correspondence from the *Field* 21 October 1876.

Commentary & Maps

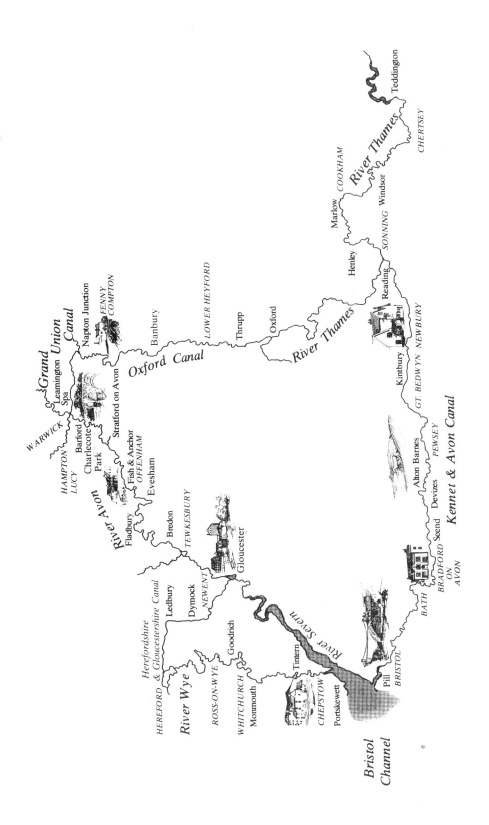

Commentary

This illustrated section is intended as a parallel commentary to the main text. It is in no way comprehensive. The references shown, e.g. 13/10 refer to page 13, line 10. References commencing RH- followed by a number, refer to the page number of *Rowing Holiday by Canal in 1873*, A. Farrant, edited by Dr. Edwin Course and published by the Oakwood Press in 1977. This is a useful comparison reference, and although not as 'wealthy' as our diarist and friends, Farrant's comments help to put the diary published here more into perspective. The route followed by Farrant and his three colleagues (all from Oxford) is exactly the same until they reach Reading, at which point they return to Oxford. The numbers shown such (1) refer to the new illustrations.

(1) The very first reference provides difficulties 15/24. '. . . and carried it on our shoulders some little distance along the line to where the railway goes over the River Cherwell . . .' From the description he gives it would appear that it was the Thames.

15/30. The Canal Pass was bought at the Canal Co. Offices, 16/1, now the site of Nuffield College.

17/1. The locks on the Oxford Canal are standard narrow locks, 72 feet long, 7 feet wide. Since Oxford Canal locks are rarely 6 feet deep, it would seem that the diarist had little previous knowledge of canals.

(2) Thrupp, 17/13.

(3) Lower Heyford, 17/25, the station and canal.

(4) The Red Lion, Lower Heyford, 17/33, now converted to cottages.

(5) Banbury Lock, 20/5. The references to barges are rather misleading as only craft over 7 foot beam are called barges, and these could not have used the Oxford Canal locks. They were, correctly, narrow boats, but in both this diary and RH they are referred to as barges.

(6) From Banbury looking north.

(7) Claydon locks, 22/2.

(8) Fenny Compton marina, alongside the site of the old railway station, 22/13.

(9) The George and Dragon, 22/16.

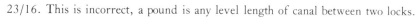

23/16. This is incorrect, a pound is any level length of canal between two locks.

(10) Napton Junction, 23/28. This is the terminus of the Oxford Canal where it joins the Grand Union Canal.

23/30. There are no locks at Napton Junction, the 'lock keeper' was in fact a toll collector.

24/18. These were standard narrow locks replaced by broad locks in the 1930s.

24/21. The lime works are referred to in RH-(14) as Nelson's Lime Works.

24/25. J. PURGIS, HAY, CORN, BRED AND COLES SOLDE HEAR. This sign is also spotted by RH-(14), but someone's memory must be at fault as they quote it as HAY AND HORS CORN LUIS, HOME BAKED BRED SOLD HEAR.

(11) Stockton Locks, 24/18.

24/35. Leamington was found to be dirty where the canal passed through, but RH-(14) stopped and walked through the town, finding it bright looking and modern.

24/36. 'The inhabitants of these houses turned out in great numbers . . .' RH-(14) experienced a similar occurrence on nearing Leamington '. . . to the great astonishment and delight of the natives, the youthful part of whom gave us a noisy welcome and the people rushed down the streets to the canal to have a look at us.'

(12) The Avon aquaduct is certainly formidable, 24/3, and as the photograph shows, it is much steeper and deeper than expressed in the line illustration on page 25. This bank was also negotiated by RH-(15).

(13) The Warwick Arms Hotel, 27/5.

(14) The monument to Piers Gaveston, 33/2. No longer visible until close up due to the woods having grown all around.

RH-(15) also had a problem at this weir, which was adjacent to a mill. They had the assistance of two men to wheel the boat around. This is an interesting coincidence as both our diarist and RH were warned at this mill of the impending shallows, 37/5.

(15) Barford Bridge. The shallows before the bridge caused a rent to be made in the boat of RH-(15), our party came to grief under the bridge itself, 38/5.

(16) The Boars Head, 39/32.

(17) Charlecote Mill, Hampton Lucy, 41/2. The mill has recently been restored to working order.

(18) Charlecote Park, 42/23, the steps leading down to the Avon are at the back.

42/25. RH-(16) also experienced trouble with this deer fence, however, they found a drop-bar and by lifting this, got through with some difficulty.

43/8. 'A tremendous crab'– to make a faulty stroke in rowing whereby the oar becomes jammed under water causing the rower to fall over backwards violently.

45/15. According to Bradshaw the Upper Avon ceased to be navigable around 1873. RH-(16) managed to open the lock, but with difficulty. Some boats were still working the river however. RH-(16) went through the lock after Luddington following a barge.

48/10. RH-(16) were able to get through at Welford after they uncovered the sluices alongside the lock. Obviously they deteriorated further in the next two years.

(19) The Upper Avon at Welford from the bridge, 48/13.

(20) Bidford on Avon, 49/8.

(21) A bend in the river at Marl Cliff Hill, 49/13.

49/14. Cleve Lock like many others has long since gone, although in some instances the site of locks on the Avon has changed.

(22) The river at Cleve.

(23) The Fish and Anchor Hotel, 50/14, presumably a much-enlarged building since 1875.

(24) The steps to the river from the Fish and Anchor, 51/4.

52/7. Offenham is not much more than a mile and a half from the Fish and Anchor.

(25) The Avon at Evesham.

54/3. '. . . we came to a lock in capital order . . .' The Avon below Evesham remained in commercial use.

(26) Fladbury Mill, 54/10.

55/3. 'We arrived at the swing sluice . . .' This was probably a flash lock.

55/12. This is Nafford Lock at Birling*ham* not Birlington.

(27) Eckington (Defford) railway bridge, showing the Bow stream meeting the Avon, 56/5.

(28) The Swan Hotel, 57/4.

(29) The Avon in Tewkesbury from the 'queer old stone bridge', 56/13.

(30) The Severn immediately below Tewkesbury. This picture looking north shows the main stream to the left leading to the ship lock, the small stream to the right with the Abbey tower as a backdrop is the Mill Avon. *See* map below.

(31) Deerhurst Church, 59/1.

(32) The Haw Bridge Inn, with a pillar of the new Haw Bridge on the right hand side. 59/3.

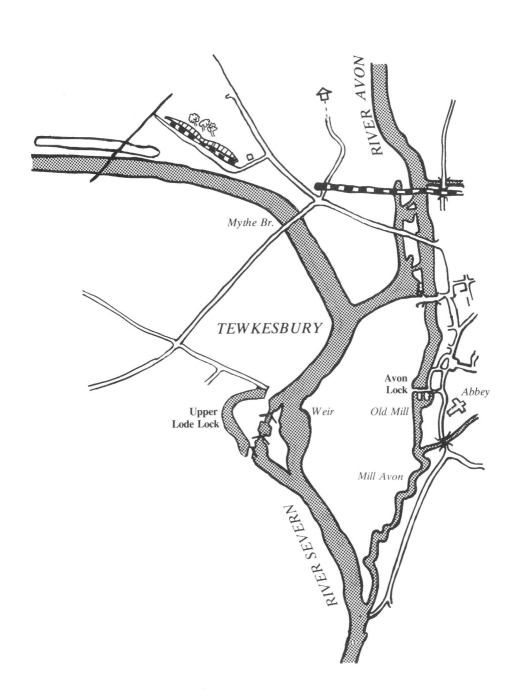

RIVER AVON

Mythe Br.

TEWKESBURY

Upper
Lode Lock

Weir

Avon
Lock

Old Mill

Abbey

Mill Avon

RIVER SEVERN

(33) The Red Lion, Wainlode, 59/8. The tides of the river never reverse the flow above this point.

(34) The Upper Parting, 59/31. *See* map below.

(35) The new railway bridge replacing the tubular bridge, 60/4.

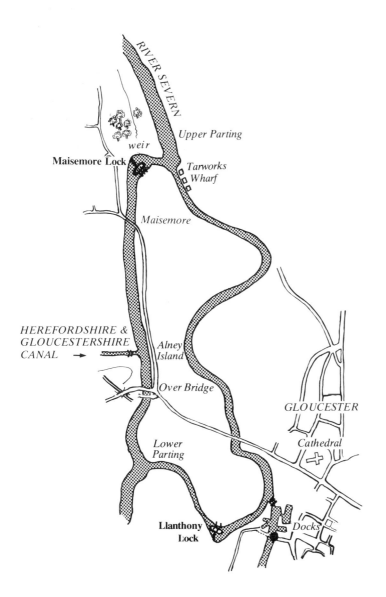

RIVER SEVERN

Upper Parting

weir

Maisemore Lock

Tarworks
Wharf

Maisemore

*HEREFORDSHIRE &
GLOUCESTERSHIRE
CANAL* →

*Alney
Island*

Over Bridge

GLOUCESTER

*Lower
Parting*

Cathedral

**Llanthony
Lock**

Docks

(36) The lock to Gloucester docks. The stream leading to Llanthony Lock and back round to Over is on the right, 60/7.

61/6. The Herefordshire and Gloucestershire Canal ownership had by this time passed to the Great Western Railway and traffic was sparse. Within a few years the canal was closed and much of the route replaced by a railway. The site of the lock at Over is now destroyed although the lockhouse still stands.

(37) The George Inn, Newent, 63/20.

62/1. Rudford Double Lock. They clearly neglected to close one or more of the bottom gate paddles.

(38 & 39) Oxenhall Tunnel, 65/15.

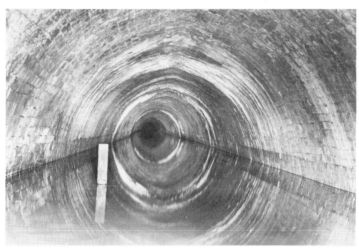

67/12. They must have moored at Bye Street at the top of the Ledbury Six Locks.

68/21. Ashperton Tunnel.

68/26. 'We went through three very deep locks . . .' Locks on the Herefordshire and Gloucestershire Canal average ten feet.

153

(40) Hereford Wharf, 68/33, the last small remains of the wharf — a stream between a timber yard and a garage.

(41) The City Arms Hotel, 69/4, now Barclays Bank Limited.

(42) The River Lugg and other tributaries flowing into the Wye, 72/27.

(43) . . . steep little hills covered with beautiful foliage extended down to the water's edge . . . 75/5.

(44) The Kings Head Hotel, 75/8.

(45) Symonds Yat, 78/10.

(46) The Ferry Inn, 78/18.

86/3. RH-22 hired a guide at Monmouth to take them down to Tintern.

(47) Chepstow Castle, 88/9.

(48) The Wye House, 88/12.

(49) James' Boatyard and the Boat Inn beyond, 88/16.

90/9. RH-(23) had planned to get across the Bristol Channel on a large boat from Tintern, but as this boat was not ready, they had to go across on the New Passage of train and steam boat, which they found very inconvenient, having to be loading and unloaded so often.

(50) The Severn Estuary, from Portskewett, 92/8.

(51 & 52) The Lamplighters Inn from Pill, 92/19.

(53) The view from the suspension bridge looking back down the Avon, 93/11.

(54) The Christopher Hotel, 97/1.

(55) This picture is a small detail from the photograph on page 98. Although all the photographs are absolutely contemporary, and bought by the diarist, his brothers and friends on the trip, the quality is superb. The resolution on this particular picture is amazing and the names on the front of the properties can easily be made out.

(56) Sydney Gardens, Bath, 100/17, *see* frontispiece.

(57) Looking across from the road, from left to right: Kennet and Avon Canal, the railway and the Avon.

(58) Dundas Aquaduct, over the Avon and the railway. Viewed from the road, 101/7.

102/18. 'We passed over another aquaduct at Stoke . . .' Avoncliffe Aquaduct.

(59 & 60) The Swan Hotel viewed from the River Avon, and from the front, 102/27.

(61 & 62) The two locks at Semington, 104/5.

(63) The Devizes flight of locks, 105/9.

(64) The Alton Barnes white horse as seen from All Cannings, 106/2.

(65) The Phoenix Hotel, 106/36.

(66) Bruce Tunnel entrance, 109/11.

110/40. '. . . and then came to ten locks all close together.' Crofton Locks.

(63) The Devizes flight of locks, 105/9.

(64) The Alton Barnes white horse as seen from All Cannings, 106/2.

(65) The Phoenix Hotel, 106/36.

(66) Bruce Tunnel entrance, 109/11.

110/40. '. . . and then came to ten locks all close together.' Crofton Locks.

(67) The Cross Keys, 111/15.

(68) Kintbury Lock, 113/13.

(69) The White Hart Hotel, now solicitors' offices, 114/7.

(70 & 71) Newbury Lock and the stone bridge beyond, 115/8.

115/17. 'The first lock we came to . . .' Greenham Lock.

115/29. RH-(26) had tremendous problems with these locks, although their first experience of them was back at Newbury, as no lock keeper seemed to be available.

(72) Blakes Lock, the last lock on the Kennet and Avon Canal, 117/27.

(73) The French Horn,
118/12.

(74 & 75) The Ferry Hotel
with the modern river front,
123/7.

(76) The Cricketers Inn (left), the Chertsey Bridge Hotel (right), 129/19.

134/1. '. . . arrived at Moulsey Lock . . .' Spelt incorrectly in the manuscript diary, should be 'Molesey'.

(77 & 78) Teddington Lock, 134/3. *See* photograph on page 133 for comparison with (77).

Acknowledgements and Editorial Note

Although labelled editorial note, the diary has not in fact been edited at all. Pains have been taken to ensure that the transcription has remained true to Howard Williams' manuscript, and any errors in place names and spellings are intentional in giving a true rendering from the diary.

Grateful thanks are due to Felicity Catmur for giving me a free hand, and for providing photographs of the route between Devizes and Teddington Lock, as well as Aubrey's Mill, Thrupp, and Charlcote Mill; David Bick for the photographs of Oxenhall Tunnel; Mark, for giving me a lift on his working boat (unfortunately one of the few), on an empty run up to Stourport, which enabled me to photograph the Severn; Michael Handford, who did the great service of introducing Felicity Catmur to the Company, and who kindly commented on the text for technical details; Martin Latham for drawing the maps; and finally to my wife Melinda, for her assistance with the photographs, and her careful attention to the production of the book.